Dr. Rawal's Definitive Guide to Financial Independence

DR. TEJINDER SINGH RAWAL

Dr. Rawal's Definitive Guide to Financial Independence

Retire Early, Retire Rich

Book Title: Dr. Rawal's Definitive Guide to Financial Independence
Book Author: Dr. Tejinder Singh Rawal

ISBN: 9798698497349
Copyright © Author Dr. Tejinder Sing Rawal 2020

Author Dr. Tejinder Singh Rawal asserts the moral right to be identified as the author of this work.

Contents

Foreword

I was lucky to find the career right for me. When I secured a top rank in my Xth grade, the family thought I will take the beaten path and would study to become a doctor or an engineer. I knew where my interest lay. I joined Chartered Accountancy to become one of the youngest Chartered Accountants in India at 21. At age 22, I was already advising my clients on the nuances of finance, investment and taxation. I continued my studies, adding diverse qualifications to my CV like M. Com, MA (Economics), MA (Public Administration), MA (English Literature), MA (Urdu Literature), LLB, Ph.D. and a plethora of professional qualifications, securing merit ranks in most of the exams I took. Nothing in this book comes from these university degrees.

I have been advising my clients on finance for over 30 years; and have lectured in universities, B-Schools, companies and institutions on various facets of finance. I have conducted courses and workshops on money and finance for school children, teenagers and young professionals. The contents of this book come from my experience and the experience of countless people who shared and discussed their finances with me. These are pearls of wisdom that will stand by you for the rest of your lives. I design this book to lead you towards Financial Independence.

When I wrote my book "Loads of Money, Guide to Intelligent Stock Market Investing" I received requests from many young friends to write a book for them which will help them create their financial-roadmap. There aren't many outstanding books written for young Indian readers. I emphasised in the earlier book that the best time to understand money was at the beginning of your career, or even before that, during your school and college education. I mean this book to fill that important gap. Money is so important to know about, that I feel this knowledge should be a part of school and university education, irrespective of your branch of study. Unfortunately, even the finance and commerce curriculum misses on this important skill and tries to teach the equilibrium theorem and the theorem of asset pricing. While these may be important concepts, the student needs something that he can put to use to create wealth for himself in the long run. If instead, we taught them to save and invest early, they might multiply the wealth that they accumulate in their later life. More importantly, they can achieve Financial Independence.

Having written, spoken, and counselled about finance all my life, I realise people know little about finance. For teaching finance to their children, people dodge the question and sometimes tell them they will know when they grow up. That is right, we expect them to learn it on their own. This explains why people often mess up their finances.

This book will be your constant companion, guiding you on every aspect of money, finance, and wealth creation. It will tell you how to find a balance between savings and spending, how and where to invest, how to get rich slow but sure way, how to set up realistic goals, and how to achieve them, how to prioritise your spending, why debt is bad for you and how to avoid getting into a debt trap, how to manage your own money, the importance of keeping a record of your transactions, how to stay away from Ponzi schemes and scams, and a host of other topics. While we primarily focus this book on young people, the philosophy applies to people of all ages.

The principles enumerated in this book are eternal and are simple to understand. And there are not many principles to master. It will surprise you to know you have to learn just a few things to create wealth. People work hard but are clueless on how to manage the money and let it grow so it serves them in later life. I hope to create many financially independent people in India so they live the life you dream of; and the fruits of the prosperity of the country are shared by a larger share of the population. The best-kept secret about finance is that there is so little to know. Unfortunately, people don't learn those simple things and regret later.

You may find many books dealing with some aspects of personal finance: books on investing, books on managing resources, books on personal finance. Unfortunately, those books do not look at the bigger picture. Life is hundreds of different aspects interconnected in a very complicated manner. All the connected parts need to be understood simultaneously. Your physical, spiritual, emotional, and financial health are interconnected so deeply that the failure of one may cause the entire system to collapse. This book draws your attention to all dimensions that will lead you to success. While the primary focus of this book is on your personal finance, as an important by-product, it makes you a better human being, a better family man and social being, and a meticulous, focused, systematic, and trustworthy person. Your life is not one aspect, but an integrated whole, and must be managed as such. This is not one of the self-help books that are written by professional authors who are often detached from the ground reality. I have lived the life I am advocating and have successfully guided hundreds of people to attain financial independence. The book is a song of experience.

As you go through the book, you discover that spending less is as important as earning more. Happiness is a state of mind that has no connection with your income level. Whatever be your present situation, you can become financially independent if you consistently follow the principles enumerated here. It works for everyone; it does not care for your background, ethnicity, present income level, or any other factor. I am not here to provide the Midas Touch. There is no new philosophy here. The book is a total of all the different aspects of personal finance that I have practised myself. It is also based on advice I have given to thousands of people during my long career in finance. I can guarantee you, they work for all without exception. After dwelling deep on various technical aspects of finance during my career, I have concluded that financial independence does not require you to do complicated things. It is nothing beyond common sense. Not many people succeed because they cannot understand that something so basic could deliver results. This book attempts to simplify not only finances but many of life's philosophies for you.

Though primarily meant for young readers, the book will serve as a personal finance guide for people of all ages. It will also be useful for financial advisers, Chartered Accountants, motivational speakers and others involved in mentoring and guiding clients.

What will this book do for you?

1.   It will change your relationship with money. You will know that money is an important constituent for successful living, but the pursuit of money as the sole aim in life may make your life miserable. Money is a good servant, but a bad master. Money is not happiness. The converse is also true.

2.   You will learn to see the road-map leading to your future. You will create goals and work towards realising those goals.

3.   You will learn the importance of saving and delayed gratification. You will understand how to put aside a portion of your income to accumulate it as a corpus which will lead you to Financial Independence.

4.   You will learn of the tiny shift in habits that make people successful.

5.   You will learn of the dangers of debts, and the beauty of a debt-free life.

5.   You will learn that living within your means is the ultimate key to financial independence.

6.   You will understand the time value of money, the power of compound interest, and will learn the basic principles that will help you make your money grow.

7.   The money will cease to be an issue in your life and you will do things that better utilise your talent and intellectual capacity.

8.   You will learn the right way to invest your money. You will know why speculation and gambling can destroy your life. You will know the right investment avenues and will know if the share market, real estate, cryptocurrencies, gold, or any other form of investment is good for you.

9.   You will learn about the money mistakes that people make.

10.   You will know of a slow but sure way of making money, and will also discover why driving in the fast lane is not the right way.

Chapter 1 Start Early

I know we don't discuss money at home. Our traditions require us to give the children the best comforts we can afford, without them realising where the money comes from, except the vague idea that papa and mommy work for some company or run a store. Beyond that, we discuss nothing at home. The topic is not taboo, but the child learns at an early age that this topic is not for discussion. We grow up without an idea about personal finance, beyond the money that we save in our piggy bank. Psychiatrists call money 'The last taboo'. We grow up as financially illiterate. The only time we discuss it when there is a crisis and the situation has gone so bad that the discussion is unavoidable.

When we enter the competitive world of education where sometimes 2 lakh students take entrance exams for 2000 seats, the chance of learning about personal finance fades even more. And we soon land in adulthood with the least idea about money.

Some people learn it the hard way by trial and error. The errors are expensive, and some blunders may cost you a fortune and in the worst case may ruin your finances. Something that should have come as a matter of routine learning, comes at a very heavy cost.

This is a sizeable gap in our education system. Not that the subject cannot be taught. The priority is often the subjects that will lead you to get admission to a university. I have scanned through the finance courses taught in various schools. They including solving problems on the computation of income using outdated income tax law provisions or archaic and irrelevant concepts of economics which neither the students nor the teacher understand, and is considered as an ordeal for both of them have to go through. They should teach personal finance at all levels, right from kindergarten to professional degree courses, and should be a compulsory part of the curriculum in schools and universities. It should become as natural to us as breathing and eating are. This book intends to fill that gap, it intends to take away the worries about personal finance from your life. You have more important things to worry about, finance should be as much a matter of routine.

Most people who discuss their finance with me are not happy with their present situation. They feel their income is not enough to cover their expenses. People do not understand that happiness does not correlate with the level of income. It depends upon how you prioritise your spending, and how well you can live within your income. Those who know the art of managing within their income are bound to live stress-free. The richest man who cannot live within his means is poorer than the poor man can do so. Happiness is not about money, it's about managing your money.

Your ethnicity, gender, family background, marital status are not relevant for attaining financial independence. Age may have some bearing because the financial needs (and, therefore, risk aversion) are different at a different stage of your life; yet the principles of financial management remain the same for you. As you shall see later, you will make your unique salad from the list of assorted greens and sauces that I will make available to you.

Kids understand money at age 3. Give a toddler a choice between one Cadbury bar now, and two bars after they finish their homework, they can test the two options. They can understand the concept of delayed gratification, which makes them understand the time value of money, an important concept in understanding the functions of money. The earlier the kids learn about money, the richer they will be in later life. Steps to become a millionaire are taken early in life. If you wait till your fifties and sixties to make you rich, you have already lost your precious time.

I always say that it's never too late to start. Start today, it is better than starting tomorrow. Even you have wasted some precious years, start NOW. The best time to plant a tree was 20 years back, the second-best is NOW.

If you understand money, life is serene. If you don't understand money life may be tough. The thing to understand is, money is not a tough thing to understand. People do not take efforts to understand it. Understanding money requires understanding many simple principles. They are all easy to understand. Assembling them into a structure requires some effort. I am here to explain to you all the things that will make you understand money; and will guide you into assembling your structure. Each one of us will build a different superstructure based on the same parts.

I understand money well and have learnt it at the School of Hard Knocks, at the University of Life. I have always felt it a social responsibility to pass on the knowledge to those with a quest for it. With this book coming to your aid, you do not have to reinvent the wheel. It needs efforts and discipline to apply these principles, but that separates a successful life from a mediocre one.

As an adviser and mentor to many people, I am often asked to tell in simple terms how to create significant wealth. There is no secret formula involved here. It is no rocket science and is one of the easiest things to understand and learn. However, it is strange that few do it. The formula is: start early. Start investing your money at the earliest; let the magic of compound interest create sizable wealth for you.

Though the price of real estate has come down considerably in recent times, for most Indians buying a house remains a difficult financial decision. It may mean committing a substantial part of your future earning also if you are considering buying a property in one of the metro cities. Children's education is an expensive affair these days, and depending on the stream chosen, it may leave you poorer by Rs 50 lakh or even more. Marriages continue to be expensive affairs in India, where people end up spending way beyond the justifiable limits. Add to this the contingencies, the medical emergencies, the lifestyle-related expenditure (foreign tours, phones, cars) and it looks like an enormous gap between saving and the required amount. While it is a daunting task, it is achievable. Invest early, earlier the better, so that the multiplier of compound interest can multiply your capital many times over. Once it gets going, the magic is unstoppable, Re 1 becomes Rs 2, 2 become 4, 4 become 8, and soon your money grows at an astonishing rate of growth, even when invested in securities that grow at a low annual rate of growth.

A young professional who has just started his career will find a low investible surplus, and he would think it is better to spend that insignificant sum instead of investing it as a small saving might not contribute much to his long term corpus requirement. This is the biggest mistake he would make. Sow the seed early, water it and I assure you, the crop you reap will be stupendous. It will be higher than his friend's returns who starts later, even if the latter invests more money.

Most people procrastinate. Some inspired by the eat-drink-and-be-merry philosophy, while many others out of ignorance. People don't know what they could do with their money, they don't realise investment options until it is too late and until it spirals into a crisis. We may see a typical procrastinator discussing a macro-economic situation which is 'grim', 'recessionary', 'bleak', or 'terrible' and is waiting for the situation to improve so he can invest. Such an opportune time never comes.

Investing early leads to Financial Independence. You may retire early while your colleagues are struggling to make both ends meet. Even if you reduce the contribution at a later stage of your life, it may not make a significant difference to your corpus, which would have grown to an impressive figure by then. Your 20 years old tree has developed enough roots and branches to stand on its own by now.

Einstein called compound interest the eighth wonder of the world and said, *"those who understand it, earn it, and those who don't pay it."* For the magic of compound interest to work, the baseline needs to reach a certain scale. Compounding is parabolic, the longer the time you give for the base to build, the higher it will take you. Few people have enough patience or foresight to realise this. If you want the magic of compound interest to work for you, you must start at the earliest and build the base early so that the ball gets rolling on its own. If you have understood the importance of compounding in the early stage of your career, nothing can stop you from becoming rich. Even modest income if invested which stays invested for a long period can make you wealthy beyond imagination.

Warren Buffett gives the example of the Mona Lisa to explain the power of compounding. King Francis I of France had asked Leonardo da Vinci to paint Mona Lisa at a cost of $ 20,000. It holds the Guinness World Record for the highest known insurance valuation in history at $100 million in 1962. This figure looks astounding until you consider that if $ 20,000 had been invested at 6% p. a., it would have grown to $1 quadrillion by 1962, 3000 times the national debt. Buffett says, "*If Francis had kept his feet on the ground and he (and his trustees) had been able to find a 6% after-tax investment, the estate now would be worth something over $1,000,000,000,000,000.00. That's $1 quadrillion or over 3,000 times the present national debt, all from 6%. I trust this will end all discussion in our household about any purchase or paintings qualifying as an investment. However, as I pointed out last year, there are other morals to be drawn here. One is the wisdom of living a long time. The other impressive factor is the swing produced by relatively small changes in the rate of compound.*"

In 1987, when I started my practice, I had purchased two computers with **MS-DOS** operating system from Wipro for Rs 45,000. (For those who are curious to know, one of them had two floppy drives, and no hard disk, you put the operating system on a floppy in drive A, and the data and application floppy in Drive B; the other one had a floppy drive and, a 10MB hard disk; the computers had a 128kb RAM) If instead of buying the computers I had bought Wipro shares for Rs

45,000 they would have been worth more than Rs 400 crores now, after considering bonus, splits, dividends and price rise!

Chapter 2 Financial Independence

The term "Financial Independence" will appear in many places in this book. Let us be clear about what we understand by the term. Financial Independence is the status of having enough income to pay one's living expenses for the rest of one's life without having to be employed or dependent on others. Financial Independence is achieved when you are not dependent upon your job to take care of your living expenses. You attain it when you have created enough passive sources of income, so you need not work to bring food to your table.

More important than your income- the often ignored component- is defining what expenditure is necessary for you. It is about defining your wants. It is about living a clean life, a life within your means. It is being satisfied with what you have.

I am not advocating the life of a monk. I am not discouraging you from earning more. This book is about maximising the return on your income and creating the best corpus you can, so you have all the money possible for you to generate. What I want you to understand is to live within your means. It is about taking a realistic stand and staying within the limit set by your income. It is about saving, say Rs 25, out of Rs. 100 you earn, until you become financially independent. It is about being happy living within Rs.75. This Rs 75 could be a different amount to different people. Financial Independence is the independence at the psychological level. You no longer have confusion about money. You are free from the slavery of money and have overcome both guilt and greed associated with money. You are free from the thoughts about money and can concentrate on higher faculties, and on things that make your life more fulfilling. You are in a state of bliss. At peace with yourself. It is not about being mega-rich, but about being happy because you are in control of the situation. You are richer than the rich person who does not know how to live within his budget.

Chapter 3 A Tiny Shift in Habits

A tiny shift in habits makes a big difference. Small change. Each change may look too small to have any impact, but when combined the cumulative effect could be the difference between success and failure. Strive to make as many changes as you can. One step at a time, till these changes become ingrained in your personality.

In his book The Power of Habit, Charles Duhigg coined the term "Keystone Habits" to describe small changes that have a powerful cascading impact on our lives. Drinking a glass of water each morning, writing what you ate once a week or five minutes of meditation each day are examples of keystone habits. So how do these small changes have such power?

By focusing on a small action that you perform often, you're able to increase your moments of victory. Getting something done feels good. Winning feels good. That emotion, even a small dose, is powerful. It can be a subtle boost, but that boost in motivation helps keep us on track. It increases our chances of succeeding at other tasks just enough to tip the scales in our favour more often than not. And for true behaviour change, consistency is the most important factor.

Nothing succeeds like success. Your original focus and effort were only on the first habit. Success in this habit built the foundation that leads to other actions. You unconsciously built other related habits. And here's the best part. These new habits grew out of the foundation you built with little to no effort. It's like magic!

Aristotle says, "We are what we repeatedly do. Excellence, then, is not an act, but a habit." Benjamin Franklin goes further to say, "Your net worth to the world is usually determined by what remains after your bad habits are subtracted from your good ones." John Maxwell says, "If your habits don't line up with your dream, then you need to either change your habits or change your dream."

I have a keen sense of observation. During my professional journey, I have observed many successful people. I have been able to find out habits that make them successful. Some of those habits are unique to those individuals, and may not be transferable. For example, some of them are heavy risk-takers. While taking a bold risk may have made them successful, that still works for some people whose composite personality such traits are a part of. Extracted, and put on another person's personality, it may produce disastrous results. I have eliminated those non-transferable skills from the list of habits to be acquired.

Every individual is unique. I am not giving you a recipe with precise measurements here. Rather, what you will acquire here are the building blocks of the popular block games that kids play with. Various combinations are possible, you need not use all blocks, but the larger is the number of blocks you use, the bigger is the structure you create.

Change your habits brick by brick. Make success a habit. When success becomes a habit, your life transforms. Be proactive. Stop hoping that a break will come, that will change your life, create that break.

The Orange Farmer

I grew up in Nagpur, a city famous for its luscious oranges (I still live in the same city). There are acres and acres of orange farms around Nagpur. Farmers in the Vidarbha region are poor, and the region is infamous for the highest number of farmer suicide in the country.

During my growing years, I would see hundreds of bullock carts loaded with oranges entering the city early morning. When it was not the orange season, the bullock carts would carry haystack. The carts would arrive at the *mandi*- the market- early morning, where the crop would be sold. By afternoon the bullock carts would be on their way back to their village. Some villages were 50-60 km away. The farmer usually loaded his produce in the night, eat the dinner, make a bed on top of the oranges or haystack and sleep while the pair of bullocks would start their journey to the *mandi*, they know the route well; they have been walking that every day of their life. One bullock cart after the other, the bullock carts from other villages join them on the way and the convoy gets bigger as it comes closer to the city.

When the farmer is old enough to travel to Nagpur, his son takes over, When the bullocks retire, a new pair will replace them, and the new bullocks will soon learn to do what their predecessors did. Day in and day out.

Now the bullock carts have been replaced by mini-trucks. But I am sure nothing in the story has changed. While I have all sympathies for the poor farmers who toil but cannot make ends meet, I wonder why some of them do not travel the extra mile. Why some of them don't think out of the box. There could be more efficient ways to reach the market, there could be better ways of selling your produce. It is a typical feature of the Indian agriculture that most profits are pocketed by the middlemen, the farmer seldom makes good money. There is usually a big difference between the price at which the produce land on your table and the price the farmer gets. If he can move slightly up the value chain and eliminate some middlemen, or get a higher share of value addition than he presently gets, his lot may improve considerably.

But he refuses to- or doesn't know how to- come out of the rut. He is in the grove and is contented there. The contentment does not allow him to think beyond his day-to-day routine, which he has been doing ever since he was born.

The reason I shared this story is that many of us also fall into a similar trap. We refuse to go beyond our comfort zone; we are grooved. If we remain in the groove, we will earn the same income that all other bullock cart farmers get. I am not judging people now, showing any apathy towards our farmers who deserve all our love and respect. I am sorry for them and wish they also gained from the fruits of development.

I shared the story so you remember it whenever you refuse to get out of your comfort zone. To succeed you will need to break that shell of inertia and move the extra mile.

The story of two wolves

We are a product of the thoughts we nurture and the habits we form. Negative thoughts can sap our energy, lose our focus, and derail us from our goals; positive thoughts can reinforce our beliefs and keeps us moving in hard times. The story of two wolves from the Navajo tribe of American Indians gives a great lesson.

An old Cherokee is teaching his grandson about life. "A fight is going on inside me," he said to the boy.

"It is a terrible fight and it is between two wolves. One is evil – he is anger, envy, sorrow, regret, greed, arrogance, self-pity, guilt, resentment, inferiority, lies, false pride, superiority, and ego."

He continued, "The other is good – he is joy, peace, love, hope, serenity, humility, kindness, benevolence, empathy, generosity, truth, compassion, and faith. The same fight is going on inside you – and inside every other person, too."

The grandson thought about it for a minute and then asked his grandfather, "Which wolf will win?"

The old Cherokee replied, "The one you feed."

We have both good wolf and bad wolf sitting inside us. Sometimes you don't even realise that you are feeding the bad wolf. The bad wolf often dulls your sense of judgment, and you derive a sense of pleasure in feeding him. You can't flush him out, you can't kill him, but you can tame him by starving. It is for you to decide which wolf to feed. Feed the right habits and they will lead you to success, feed the wrong ones, and you move away from your target.

Chapter 4 Don't Gamble

If you are one of those who think you can make it big by gambling or at a casino, read this. Know the basic rule: the house always wins. Casinos and lotteries make a profit by offering games of chance where the average payouts are lower than the income produced by the overall wagers. That is how the bets are organised.

The probability of winning at gambling is ridiculously low. The probability of winning a jackpot could be remote. We overestimate the probability of winning. One in a Million looks like a winning odd to many. Human irrationality is at work when calculating the winning probability of winning versus the probability of getting killed in a road accident. People know that they are unlikely to win a lottery and they are unlikely to die in a road accident. They do not know how unlikely. If they could calculate the probability of winning a lottery and of an accident, they will know that the chances of dying in a road accident are 50 times higher than the probability of winning the jackpot in the Maharashtra State lottery. If you can understand this simple math, you will drive more carefully, and will not buy lottery tickets. When asked to estimate the probability of a rare positive event, people estimate it too high.

If you are still not convinced, consider the following probabilities:

The probability of having identical quadruplets: 1 in 15 million

The probability of someone becoming a Bollywood star: 1 in 5 million

The probability of someone dying in a plane crash or being struck by lightning: 1 in 1 million

When you buy a lottery ticket sold to 15 million people (State government Diwali special and new year special) the probability of you winning it is not more than the probability of you having identical quadruplets!!

If you do not want to understand the mathematics behind it, just take my words: you will not win at a lottery. Even if you are one in a million who wins by the act of randomness, the gamble is not worth your time and effort. Please do not gamble, neither at a casino, nor at a slot machine, nor any online lottery, nor legalised government-controlled lottery.

Even if you won the lottery, you might not hold on to the money. One of the first things many people do after receiving their newfound financial freedom is to quit their job. It's also natural to go on a spending spree, after all now you have more money than you ever imagined, and you did not toil to earn that money: a fancy new house, a new car, a luxury vacation. And then, maybe, help friends, family, colleagues—everyone you've ever known will come out of the woodwork asking for help. Drastically elevating expenditures, ceasing to earn income, gifts, and handouts—it's no small wonder so many lottery winners eventually end up in financial distress.

Though not a lottery in the conventional sense of the term, I have seen the plight of people who got similar windfall: the farmers who once owned agricultural land closer to cities and highways. Because of urbanisation the land value went up by 100x, and they sold the land (no longer agricultural, but the prime urban property now) at an unbelievable price. To them, this was nothing less than a lottery. When some of them got a notice from the tax department a couple of years later for paying taxes on the capital gains (they were so poor earlier, they didn't even know that taxes existed) and they came to our office for advice; we were shocked to find that they had squandered away the windfall, and they were as poor as they always were, owning some white elephants like a large house and a car which made their situation more pathetic than earlier.

If you win a gamble, it tempts you to bet more and increase the stake. Greed has no end, and the temptation to make a quick buck without efforts is irresistible. Before you realise it, you have already become an addict. It becomes difficult to break the habit. People beg, borrow, or steal to gamble. Gambling gives them the same kick that drugs give. The endgame is disastrous. There is no such thing as "I know my limits." Or "I am gambling fun sake.". Remember gambling = drugs.

You may lose your shirt to gambling. I know people who lost everything and died a pauper. I know people who lost everything and went into acute depression or committed suicide. Gambling may destroy relationships and may tear your family and life apart.

If you are one of those who have unlimited supplies of money (though this is impossible, to a man who gambles, no amount of money is enough) use that money for better use. Give it to charity, spend it on educating people, spend it on purposes that will make the world remember you as someone who made a difference.

Chapter 5 Live Within Your Means

It is commonsense that saving is the difference between your income and expenditure. Whatever be your income, if you live within it, you save. If your expenditure exceeds your income you are in trouble.

I love to quote Mr. Micawber from Charles Dickens' David Copperfield, 'Annual income twenty pounds, annual expenditure nineteen nineteen six, result happiness. Annual income twenty pounds, annual expenditure twenty pounds nought and six, result misery."

Live within your means. This is the first principle you should master. You cannot move to the next level unless you commit yourself to this. Know how much to spend out of your money. In no case shall you spend money that you don't have.

Success demands commitment, without commitment you won't go far. I will handhold you, I just need a promise from you, you will commit the time and energy I demand of you.

In the world of consumerism, where credit is readily available, it is easy to falter. Spend money only if you have it in your pocket. Learn to save first and spend out of your savings. This habit gained early in life will be your biggest strength in future life. People who fail to live within their means are doomed to failure.

Living within your means is easier said than done. In a world where you want to flaunt brands, you are wearing or owning, want to show off your expensive smartphone and trendy car, and want to be seen at the best of places; you succumb easily. It requires a great deal of courage to stay disciplined in the face of temptation. Stop thinking of what others think of you, and you have won half the battle. Living within your means does not mean you have to live on a shoestring budget. It only means you must live within the limits of your finances, undeterred by what others think or might think of you.

If you want to buy the latest gadget, save, save enough to let you buy the gadget without affecting your finances. Before you buy any product or service, ask yourself the purpose that purchase will serve. Do I need it? What are the other options? If I postpone my buying decision, what effect will it have?

In the fast-changing world of technology, what you buy today will be cheaper tomorrow, it may also go obsolete soon. Evaluate if you need something. Justify every purchase that you make. Before you spend every rupee, think. Companies want you to be impulsive. That's why you see tempting goods at the check-out counters of supermarkets. Intelligently designed product advertisements from Amazon or your favourite online vendor pop out to catch your attention. Companies want you to store your credit card details on their website so that once you click the buy button, the money is gone forever from your account. Think twice, thrice, four times before you commit to buy.

Have you noted media and the government refers to you as 'consumer'? You are not a person or a citizen, but a consumer. You are someone with money who must be tempted to part with it. They make every effort to take every penny out of your pocket. People are trained to do that, targeted advertisements are employed for the purpose. It requires discipline and knowing your priorities to protect yourself from this legal scam.

Do not buy things until they wear out or until you know you can't do without them. Look for discounts and bargains, if planned properly you can save a great deal of money. One of the richest men in the world, Warren Buffett, who consumes Cherry Coke as his staple drinks buys the coke cans in bulk from the wholesale stores, since they sell it cheap there. Know well what you want and what you don't want. Know thyself.

To have savings is to have freedom. Your boss may fire you, your business may go bad, the sky may fall (yes, it does, proof: COVID-19), if you have money in your bank, you may buy land, you may buy investments that make your savings grow, you may survive the sudden disruption, you may start a new business, you may pay your EMI when you are not receiving your paycheques. Saving is a means of stress-free living.

The worst debt is credit card debt. The visible and invisible charges put together make this the most expensive debt. Use credit cards with caution, develop the habit of living within your means. Never spend money that you don't have. Do not borrow from the future. The future may come with its own set of liabilities. Stay within your means.

Downsize Wedding

In India marriage is a big thing. People spend way beyond their resources at weddings. The following statistics will shock you.

1.   People spend as much as 10 times their annual income on weddings.

2.   Weddings are a big part of India's GDP. One bridal dress of a middle-class bride may cost up to one month's income of the family. The bride must have half a dozen dresses for different occasions.

3.   It is not unusual for three generations of relatives to come from far and near. Their stay must be hosted in the best hotel the family can afford.

4.   The latest fad of pre-wedding shoots is like a mini-movie that costs a bomb.

5.   80% of Indians take loans for weddings. It takes around 5 years to pay back the loans. The family income of the next five years gets committed towards repayment of the wedding loan. Such loans are personal loans on which a high rate of interest is charged. Some people take loans from friends and family, and moneylenders.

The wedding function is over in 1-3 days. The money evaporates. People go back home, and the story is soon forgotten, as people get busy preparing for another marriage in the family. There is no societal pressure, no compulsion on how much you should spend in marriage. People spend because they want to impress the relatives and the community. Nobody gets impressed, nobody bothers.

You will do a great service to yourself by scaling down the wedding. Save the money, and use it to kick-start investment, or use it as a down payment to buy a house if you don't own any. Or invest the money in equities, it may grow into a big sum.

I know one thing for sure, marital bliss does not correlate with the amount of money spent on wedding festivities. If you budget your marriage properly and invest the money wisely, it may be the beginning of a happy married life with the right philosophy.

If marriages are made in the heavens, why do we spend so much money to celebrate it on earth? Marriage is often the biggest unproductive expenditure of your life. Curtail.

Get Health Insurance

Health insurance is an important component of your financial planning that you cannot ignore. With the fast increasing cost of medical treatment in our country, and the increasing health risk arising out of lifestyle diseases, and attack of unknown viruses, it is unwise to remain uninsured. An accident is an accident, it does not come with a previous warning. It will not only save you a lot in terms of financial consequence should something go wrong, but will also make your life stress free, once you know that all insurable risks in your life are covered.

Read the policy document carefully before you sign the cheque. Does your insurance offer cashless benefits? If not, you may have to pay to the hospital first, the money will be reimbursed to you later.

Does it cover pre and post hospitalisation expenses? What ailments does it cover? Is the coverage wide enough to cover all conceivable ailments and injuries?

You can also evaluate buying a critical insurance policy as an add-on to the main policy. The critical illness policy provides for paying you a fixed sum of money should a critical illness specified in the policy is diagnosed. This may act as a replacement of a source of income in the event of a critical illness which may significantly impair your income earning potentials.

You may also consider buying a life insurance policy. Term insurance usually works best for young adults. The statistical probability of a young person dying is low, so the premium payable based on the actuarial calculations is very low. Go for a longish term policy at a young age and the premium payable will be low and affordable.

Chapter 6 Waste Not, Want Not

We are reaping the fruits of industrialisation and mass production. Production in the era before the Industrial Revolution was a tiresome process. One of the greatest economists and thinkers of all times, Adam Smith (1723-1790)- appropriately called the Father of Economics- gives an example of pin-making. He argued that the main cause of prosperity was an increasing division of labour. He asserted that ten workers could produce 48,000 pins per day if each of the eighteen specialised tasks was assigned to particular workers. Average productivity: 4,800 pins per worker per day. But absent the division of labour, a worker would be lucky to produce even one pin per day.

Computerisation and automation made the process even faster, and now one machine can churn out millions of pins on its own unattended by any supervisor. This has made pins cheaper and we are free to waste pins by hundreds. Before the mass production pins were so precious that the allowance given to the women by their husbands was called 'the pin money'.

One historian writing on the history of the Colonial days Bombay (now Mumbai) said that people wearing shoes and watches were too few and were among the richest people in the city. Now it is not uncommon for people to buy enough shoes and sandals to match each of the dresses. We can have the wristwatch for the price of one meal at a fast-food joint.

Ideally, this should have increased your savings, which could have been added to the capital that grows over time. Unfortunately, the story does not have a happy ending. We buy dozens of watches and shoes and clothes and everything else, only to throw them away when you don't want to wear them any longer. The actor turned politician Jayalalithaa had 10,500 saris, 750 pairs of slippers, and 500 wine glasses!

Cheaper goods mass-produced makes them affordable. We can buy more does not mean we should buy more. Take care of your stuff.

Keep your belongings in good condition. Maintain your bicycle/scooter/car well and it will last longer and will remain more dependable. Keep your furniture and apartment in good repair. Regular upkeep enhances the working life of your assets. Maintain your clothes well and they last twice as long. Have a place for your belongings, and keep them at their designated place, so they are not 'lost' when you need them. There should be "a place for everything, and everything in its place", as they say. The bonus is that the well-maintained house with everything neat and tidy brings you accolades from friends and family.

A Pin for Gandhi

Mahatma Gandhi used to get not only fan mail but a lot of hate mail too. One day he received a long abusive letter from a man he hardly knew. The letter ran into five pages and they had been put together with a pin. When Gandhi had finished reading the letter, he took out the pin, carefully kept it on his table and threw the pages into the wastepaper basket. A visitor who was sitting there asked him why he had taken out the pin. Gandhi thanked the sender and replied, "It was the only useful thing in the letter".

Chapter 7 Find Good Friends

Who your friends are in your formative years has a considerable bearing on your financial success in later life. Good friends impact your mental, physical and emotional health. Lack of social connection may pose serious risks associated with a sedentary lifestyle. Friends are tied to your longevity. Research has shown that those who have enduring social bonds live longer and healthier.

But friendship does not happen overnight. It is the building of a trust relationship that gradually grows and requires time and effort.

Friends act as your support system. They lift your spirits when you are low or down. If you are tense or stressed up, friends can help you overcome that.

When you are trying to reach a financial goal, or quit a bad habit or lose weight, friends can provide great support. They increase your willpower and may create favourable situations for you.

Just having someone willing to listen to you and share your problems may mean a lot to come out of depression or troubling situations.

As you grow, you will find people willing to network with you, but most of those relationships will be give-and-take relationships, built not on trust but on mutual benefits. The real friendship usually develops in the initial periods of your life, when people have no vested interest nor any baggage to carry. Such friendships last long and provide comfort and succour when you need them.

Friendship demands commitment. It is a two-way street. The way you expect your friends to stand by you in the moments of joy and sorrow, the friends also expect it to be reciprocated. Be prepared to travel the extra mile to help a friend in distress and to ease their suffering. The bonds of friendship need continuous nourishment to grow stronger.

Friendship requires you to be a better listener. Learn to listen to others with patience. There are very few in this world with that rare talent. People are becoming lonely because there is nobody to listen to them. Speak less and listen more and you will develop great friendships.

We make friends at places where we cross paths with people. Schools, colleges, gyms, libraries, coffee shops, places of worship, and other hangout places are the usual places. A friendship develops faster and stronger when you have a common interest with the person. Shared hobby, career path, heritage, cultural background, ethnicity are often the things that bring people closer.

Volunteering often helps. It brings out the caring and sharing traits. Find volunteering opportunities wherever you can. Give to the world, you shall get rewarded in terms of some of the best friends you make there.

Join a club that caters to your interest and age group. Clubs are the best networking places. Jaycees, Lions, Rotary, Masonic Lodge, Round Table are some of the best places to meet new people who will know you and to extend the hand of friendship to you,

Unplug! It is impossible to connect to the people around you if you have created a digital barrier. If you are busy on your cell phone or social media account, you are restricting access to potential friends around you. Learn when not to use your cell phone and the Internet. Do not sacrifice real friendship at the altar of fake on-line friendship.

If you are too busy and don't have time to meet people, put it on your calendar. Schedule a Meetup. Mix business, sports, or hobbies with pleasure. I have made many friends during my bike ride and runs. My monthly Book Club is great for renewing my bonds of friendship with my bibliophile friends. I have made great friends of all ages in hundreds of training programs, seminars, and conferences I have spoken at.

Don't be afraid of rejection. For a better friendship, be a better friend yourself. Be prepared to give more than you receive. Be a good listener. People love to tell stories but do not find patient ears. Lend that ear, and you will make a friend for life. Be forgiving. People make mistakes and need to be forgiven In friendship, do not make mountains out of molehills. You should ignore the shortcomings of your friends and move on. Life is too short to be critical of the people around you.

It is perfectly all right to seek help from your friends. People love to help others and seek help, and it is bound to come. Sometimes advice may come from people you thought could never help. An outsider to the transaction has the advantage of sitting outside the scene and can analyse and interpret more objectively. Just make sure you are not swayed by their decisions and are only taking inputs from them. Learn to talk to people and take their inputs and take your own reasoned decision after that.

The habit of seeking help will stand you in great stead in your later life. As one gets older one gets more reluctant to seek advice. Unless one has inculcated the art in earlier stages.

Your Inner Circle

Show me your friends and I will show you your future. The Bible says, "He that walketh with wise men shall be wise: but a companion of fools shall be destroyed."

Who are your friends? Who are the people you move around with? Who are the people who influence you or are influenced by you? In short, who is your inner circle? Show me those people and I can predict where will you be a few years from now. Some people give negative vibes, they think pessimistic in every situation; they feel that the world out there is bad, and try to find fault with everything and everybody. They find a world full of conspiracies.

Being conservative differs from being pessimistic. Acting as devil's advocate and doing a SWOT analysis of the situation is not bad, but if someone looks at only the negative side in everything around, and if that person is a part of your inner circle, there is a problem.

If you believe you have negative friends but that does not affect you, you are wrong. You may shun them once or twice, but you do not realise that they are influencing you invisibly. I know it may not be possible to stay away from some relations. Some relations are 'given' to you and are unavoidable. You may, however, try to influence them with your positivity instead of getting influenced by their negativity. I have a workaround to handle the situation.

Try to analyse the people around you. List out people who give you positivity, and those who drain your positivity. When you meet a stranger, usually during the first few conversations, you can find out if the person is positive or negative for you. Having categorised people as a positive influence and a negative influence, it's time to define your inner circle. Only positive influencers have a place in your inner circle. Others are out of it, even if you shake hands with them daily. Define your circle. The circle has to be taken seriously, others remain out of it. But they are not to be ignored. Influence them. Thanks to social media we all understand the terms 'influencer' and 'follower' well. Try to be an influencer to the people around you but out of your inner circle. Guard against their negativity influencing you and make every effort to influence them with your positive influence. If you can improve the situation of people around you by spreading your positive influence, you will have more successful people around you, and you will be proud that it is you who sowed the seeds of success in them. The ways to influence others can be many. To those who listen to you, speak. To those who do not influence by your conduct. Your good habits should show, they should reflect on your conduct. If they do, it is difficult for others not to get influenced. The formula here is to ignite your light so bright that the light of the negative influence looks dim in comparison.

Chapter 8 Learning at the University of Life

Your first few jobs are a great learning university where they are paying you to learn. You will get more than you are giving to build skills that will last a lifetime. Put your heart and soul into it.

Grab every opportunity of working for others. Treat each job as something that adds a new dimension to your persona. Volunteering has great learning potentials too.

While most of your friends will consider it not worthy to put in more hours than the mandated minimum in their jobs ("Why should I give more when they are paying me low?") always be ready to travel that extra mile. Go beyond the call of duty. As an adult, you will never get such opportunities. Ask for more challenges, more opportunities to contribute to your knowledge base.

Jobs are the universities of real knowledge. All jobs comprise people skills. Knowledge gained in the university is only 20% of what you do at your job. Rest comes from communication and dealing with people. You will get used to working with the people you like; you will also get used to working with people you dislike.

In your first job you quickly realise that if you want to stand apart and distinguish yourself, you must take initiative. Employees wait for the orders, those who take initiative rise to the top.

You will learn by making mistakes. Don't be afraid. You make mistakes, correct them, and move to the next level. This is how the learning curve operates. Employers prefer employees who make mistakes, learn, and improve over employees who do not do things they have not done before for the fear of making mistakes.

Use your job to expand your circle of competence. Expertise gets rewarded in the long run, money, and success comes out of the knowledge and competence you gain. Have an indefatigable quest for knowledge. As the Vedas say, आः नो भद्राः क्रतव्यो यन्तु वश्वितः let noble thoughts come to us from the whole universe.

Invest in your future. Learn all that you can about personal finance. Learn about the stock market, mutual funds, real estate market, personal taxation, financial goals, and wealth creation. Spend an hour daily. Nurture this as a hobby. The time you spend on watching TV every day, if spent on learning personal finance, can make you a finance wizard. It surprises me to find people spending so much time updating themselves on the score of their favourite cricket player. If you spent half of that time learning about personal finance, you will retire early and will have a lot of time at your disposal to update the cricket score. This is not to discourage you from having hobbies, but to exhort you to find a balance between leisure and personal growth.

Keep looking for programmes and resources that enhance your finance skills. There are ample resources available on the Internet for you to learn personal finance from. Financial newspapers like the Economic Times and Financial Express and magazines like Business Today and Forbes are great resources. Look for seminars and workshops that teach you the skills. Find mentors who can guide you. There is no dearth of resources for someone willing to learn. As the Bible says, "Ask, and it shall be given you; seek, and ye. shall find; knock, and it shall be opened unto you."

Start spending an hour daily on learning personal finance. Over your lifetime you would have invested thousands of hours that will make you an expert in the subject. It requires thousands of hours of practice to make you an expert in any field. A qualified Chartered Accountant who stops learning after qualifying stagnates. A non-finance professional who spends an hour a day consistently improving his knowledge can put themselves ahead of the qualified professionals.

Look at the richest people in the country. While some of them were born with a silver spoon, most of them had a humble beginning. India is a land of opportunity, one of the fastest-growing economies in the world. If you have an idea and a serious determination to succeed none can stop you. Dhirubhai Ambani once sold *bhajias* at fairs and worked at a petrol pump. He rose to become the greatest wealth creator of modern India. The founder of Rs. 7000 crores Nirma group Karsanbhai Patel was born in a family of farmers and once worked as a lab assistant. A college dropout Gautam Ambani went to Mumbai with little money to start his business at age 18. His wealth is estimated to be over 7 billion dollars. Dharampal Gulati, one of the most well-known faces in Indian ads, the owner of MDH Masale was a refugee who came penniless during the partition of India. He drove a tonga in Delhi to make a living. He started making spices in a 14'x9' room. His company is the biggest name in the spice industry now.

Satya Nadella, the CEO of Microsoft puts it thus, "Always keep learning. You stop doing useful things if you don't learn. So the last part to me is the key, especially if you have had some initial success. It becomes even more critical that you have the learning 'bit' always switched on.

Chapter 9 Make Money Slowly

"Get rich quick" is too good to be true. Less than 1 in 1,000 get rich that way. This book is not about making you an overnight millionaire. If you came here with that intention, you are likely to be disappointed.

This book promises you unimaginable riches, but they come slowly over time. The way most millionaires have created their wealth. Slow but sure way.

Even bountiful inheritance vanishes in no time unless you know the skills of managing money. Those with the know-how and a little money can rise to the top if they are willing to start early and systematically build wealth. Start early, spend less, save more, avoid conspicuous consumption, and invest wisely. There is no other way.

Start saving and investing when you have nothing to invest. This may look absurd, but the fact is, scarcity teaches big lessons which life of abundance does not. Enjoy the life lived within your means and save something out of the scarce resources that you have. While it may not be a big sum of money, it is meant to instil discipline in you. The discipline that will help you when your income and savings eventually grow.

I am not here to give you a one-size-fits-all formula. Rather, you will create your wealth making principles under the guidance of this book. You will create your money code, and will enjoy the journey to the riches. You will enjoy the journey more than the destination. There is no fixed destination to stop. Once you enjoy the journey, you keep setting goals, reach them, and move on to set another goal, and so on. The rewards of this journey are much more than the actual money you make.

The founder of Zara Amancio Ortega knew how to make wealth the slow and sure way. Son of a railway worker, he started working at an early age as a worker in the textile industry to support his family. To feed his family, he sacrificed on education, and never received an education beyond secondary school. Working as a shirt maker he learnt the intricacies of fashion designing. He was always inquisitive and liked to know different elements of costs involved in making a shirt out of cloth and reaching it to the final consumer. He worked for 10 years, learning every aspect of manufacturing, raw material procurement, quality control, sales and marketing, cont control, brand building, accounting and finance, employee motivation, and human relations. Finally, he was ready to launch his own business. By now he knew what the customers wanted. His company Confecciones Goa, selling bathrobes, became an instant hit with the customers. 12 years later, after establishing sufficient credibility in the market, he was ready to launch his consumer brand Zara. Zara is an agile company, which is always the first company to recognise changing fashion trends in the market. While others are trying to research the market, Zara ships out the latest trends. And it does so in the most cost-effective manner. The deep knowledge of Ortega helped him inculcate that culture in his company. Another unique feature of Zara is that they never mass produce their high-end products. They make sure every elite customer can boast of a design unique to him. So much to satisfy the egos of those who are willing to may the moon for clothes and accessories.

Zara later opened stores all over the world, making Ortega one of the richest men in the world. Rich, he may be, but he loves to remain as low profile as he can. He avoids giving interviews, does not like to be photographed. It is said he has not taken a holiday for 25 years. So much dedication, and so much he enjoys his work.

Chapter 10 Set Realistic Goals

The first step towards becoming financially secure is to set your short term and long term financial goals. Unless you have a road-map, you would not know where are you going.

Think big. Most of the people who have made it big could do so because they knew they could do it; they believed they could do it. Many of us refuse to tune to the right channel. We don't dream of ourselves wealthy; the obvious result is that we never grow rich because we never planned for it. You need to condition your mind into believing you are wealthy and successful. This is the precondition: unless you believe you can do it, you can't do it.

Set your goals. We procrastinate. Even if we know something could be good for us, we delay it. The income tax department understands this psychology. They know the bulk of income tax returns are furnished on the deadline. And the remaining on the extended deadline. In personal finance, often there is no deadline from outside. Your credit card company is happy when you do not pay the debt in time, as long as they are confident of your creditworthiness. The delay is expensive. Not investing in time is equally expensive in terms of less wealth-creation.

A fool and his money are soon parted because the fool does not define his goals. Unless you define where you want to go, you will never reach there. This is very important. Set your goals. You need to create your mission statement, and then based on such a statement, define your goals, both long term, and short term. Your goals should be quantifiable. 'I want to be rich' is not a defined goal. (Who doesn't want to be rich?) 'I want to have a net-worth of Rs. 1 crore by age 35' is a goal.

While the former is just a wish, the latter put a quantified value to it, and you can measure your performance as you move towards achieving your goal. The best way to define and quantify your goal is to write it down. Write it down clearly and unambiguously as if you are writing work specifications.

Doing things without setting your goals is like driving a fast SUV on an expressway at the speed of 100 km per hour, not knowing where you are going. You will keep going till you run out of gas and will be stranded in the middle of nowhere. Before you embark on a journey of life, look at the map, and set the mental GPS to take you to the next destination.

It is strange to see so many men and women driving their life in 'Ferrari' mode but with GPS off. They don't realise that while they think they are moving, they are running on a treadmill. Look at the mirror, are you one of them?

Set the goal that will make you exert yourself. If you set your target too low, it will fail to be an effective motivation. Your goal should cause a little discomfort, a little stress, which produces positive results. It should be realistic, though it must be set a notch higher than your present capability. Setting a goal that is far too unrealistic will defeat the purpose. If you are setting an impossible goal, you are likely to throw it out of the window sooner than later.

Benjamin Franklin was one of the most accomplished men throughout history. All his life he used a 'goal system' that he first devised when 20 years of age, which he wrote about in his memoirs. First published as "The Autobiography of Benjamin Franklin" in 1791, Mr. Franklin wrote of his method to establish habits to achieve the following 13 life goals, which he called the thirteen virtues:

"TEMPERANCE. Eat not to dullness; drink not to elevation."
"SILENCE. Speak not but what may benefit others or yourself; avoid trifling conversation."

"ORDER. Let all your things have their places; let each part of your business have its time."

"RESOLUTION. Resolve to perform what you ought; perform without fail what you resolve."

"FRUGALITY. Make no expense but to do good to others or yourself; i.e., waste nothing."

"INDUSTRY. Lose no time; be always employ'd in something useful; cut off all unnecessary actions."

"SINCERITY. Use no hurtful deceit; think innocently and justly, and, if you speak, speak accordingly."

"JUSTICE. Wrong none by doing injuries, or omitting the benefits that are your duty."

"MODERATION. Avoid extremes; forbear resenting injuries so much as you think they deserve."

"CLEANLINESS. Tolerate no uncleanliness in body, cloaths, or habitation."

"TRANQUILLITY. Be not disturbed at trifles, or at accidents common or unavoidable."

"CHASTITY. Rarely use venery but for health or offspring, never to dullness, weakness, or the injury of your own or another's peace or reputation."

"HUMILITY. Imitate Jesus and Socrates."

To keep track of his adherence to these goals, Franklin carried around a small book of 13 charts. The charts comprised a column for each day of the week and 13 rows marked with the first letter of his 13 virtues. Franklin evaluated himself at the end of each day. He placed a dot next to each virtue each had violated. The goal was to minimise the number of marks, thus showing a "clean" life free of vice.

Franklin would especially focus on one virtue each week by placing that virtue at the top of that week's chart and including a "short precept" to explain its meaning. Thus, after 13 weeks he had moved through all 13 virtues and would then start the process over again.

When Franklin first started on his program, he found himself putting marks in the book more than he wanted to. But as time went by, he saw the marks diminish.

At 20, he recognised that distractions and bad habits stood in the way of achieving his goals, and created a system to overcome them. For 50 years, he held himself accountable in this system to build the life he desired.

Benjamin Franklin's one goal system with notebooks, a ruler, and pen helped him to become one of our most prolific inventors, Statesmen, writers, scientists, and entrepreneurs.

Read and re-read your goals periodically. Compare the actual results with the projected. See how you are faring. If you are performing better than expected, is it time to revise your targets upwards? If you are performing poorly, are things going wrong, or do you need to lower your expectations?

Do not have too many goals. Setting too many goals may confuse you and you may lose focus. Goals may often contradict each other and may lead to dilemma situations. Keep them simple, keep them short, and keep them limited to the things you want.

Your goal should be measurable, you should be able to track and measure your progress. They should be tangible. You should be able to visualise them. If you can visualise something, the chances of success are higher. Abstract goals get lost in the oblivion.

You may lose sight of your long term goals easily since you often focus on the short-term issues and problems at hand. Create ambitions but attainable goals after doing a thorough assessment of your strengths and weaknesses. It is very important to recalibrate your goals periodically as you achieve (or cannot achieve) short-term and medium-term milestones.

Short term financial goals give you the confidence boost needed to achieve the long term goals and should be regarded as the building block of long term goals. If your long-term goals are like a marathon run, short-term goals are 5k, 10k, and 21k distances where you can test your performance and recalibrate your timings.

As a component of your short-term goal, you may make a daily or weekly budget. This will help you understand what you spend on food and clothing, and other items of consumption. Few people know these statistics. This will be an important step towards self-discovery.

Create an emergency fund. Emergencies are emergencies. They come without warning. Create a corpus to take care of sudden disruptions and emergencies. As I write this chapter, Corona Virus is affecting millions and is causing a major global recession. Keep funds for such situations. As you recalibrate your long term goals from time to time, you will simultaneously need to review your emergency corpus too. My suggested criteria for the emergency fund is a sum that can support you for at least six months if you had no income. Build it up gradually.

Your mid-term goals may include repaying your student loan, getting yourself sufficiently insured, buying a house, and starting a family. There are no fixed milestones, decide which goals are important to you. While you do that, keep adding to your emergency corpus. Once you have set up your midterm goals, it is time to dream big. It is time to fine-tune your long term goal. Visualise the future you would like to give to yourself, and that will be the first step towards achieving it.

Your children's education from early education to college could be the next goal. Conventional wisdom suggests less aggressive asset allocation, meaning adding debt component (bonds, fixed deposits or any other interest-bearing securities), and analysts give a ballpark allocation of 60:40 or similar. This generalisation may not help in your case, and my suggestion here does not differ from the earlier: keep investing as much in equity as possible.

Retirement planning has to continue to be important all your working life. You need to keep adjusting your goal in the light of changing circumstances so that your investment remains worthwhile. One important factor to be considered here, though often ignored, is that the life expectancy is on the rise. The average life expectancy in India is around 70. If you are an educated urban dweller with good hygiene standards, and access to good medical facilities, you are likely to live much longer. Those who allocate a higher portion of their assets to bonds in their forties and fifties often face a situation where inflation eats into their principal. Being risk-averse, they move away from 'risky' equities into the 'safe haven' of fixed-income securities only to find that the capital may not last their lifetime. The conventional wisdom fails here too. The best solution is to invest early, invest in inflation-beating asset classes like equity, and stay invested as long as possible. I will keep reiterating at the cost of repetition that equity as an asset class if invested following the principles enunciated in this book, would not fail. Equity, in the long run, is safer than bonds.

If you are at a stage of your life where the mortgage has been paid off, and all your major liabilities (In the Indian context it may also include children's marriage) have been taken care of, it is time to review your retirement corpus. If there has been a drain or some shortfall, it is time to top it up. The best strategy is to invest early, so you don't have to provide top-up allocation later, yet it makes sense to review the situation at the availability of additional funds, and add to it when you need to.

Succession planning should go hand in hand with wealth creation. Draw a will and define how your estate will be distributed after you. This process should start at an early stage of your life and should be reviewed every few years.

The long term goal should include the planning for retirement, and the creation of an alternate source of income and wealth growth, besides your day job.

A rule of thumb: at least 10-15% of all you earn should be set aside and invested for your future. As your disposable income grows, you may up this proportion, which would mean investing a bigger chunk of a bigger cake. Some people have lived frugally and invested as much as 80% of their income sleeping in a car and eating food that gives the highest calorie per rupee. They saved everything, invested, and retired early. While I do not recommend this extreme approach, the choice is entirely yours.

You may not make linear straight progress towards the achievement of your goals. You cannot achieve some targets, while you would reach others earlier than expected. If you are required to spend on a hefty medical bill one month and end up drawing from your emergency corpus instead of adding to it; do not despair. As long as you are heading towards your goals, even in a crisscross manner, like the walk of a drunken man, it is perfectly fine.

Before you proceed to the next chapter, take a notepad or a digital notepad, and describe your present situation, and write about where you want to be. Do not think of other people's perceptions of you. Look at the mirror and think of the real you, you in your perception.

You are lucky to be living in that phase of history where the potentials to grow is unlimited. (I am writing this at the peak of the COVID 19 pandemic, knowing fully well that we shall overcome it.) The only limitation is the lack of vision and road-map. Focus visualise and plan systematically. Nothing can stop you from being successful.

A good visualisation exercise is to 'look back from the future'. Visualise that you have reached your dream destination, now look back to think of all milestones that brought you there. This will help you plan better. Instead of going from point A to point B, imagine you are already at point B, now write the steps that enabled you to reach that point by rewinding your the story in your imagination

Chapter 11 Invest Incremental Income

Once you have learnt to live within means and control your inflows and outflows, as and when you get an extra income, a bonus, a bounty, a windfall, a gift from an uncle, or anything that was not a part of your budget, invest at least half of that amount. The extra money that came your way was not anticipated. While you will have a temptation to celebrate by burning that money, keeping a ready plan to invest that extra income will help. Always keep thinking of where will you invest if you had more money, even when you do not have money at hand so that when the money lands in your hands, you do not spend it on things that give you immediate gratification but does not create any wealth for you.

If you are an employee, you may apply this rule to the increments. At least half of the increments in salary should go towards creating wealth for your future.

This step is an easy way of generating wealth. So simple, I wonder why don't many people do it. The reason people fail to invest the extra income is that they have no game plan. They do not see the bigger picture. They have not done the homework on how they would spend the money if they had it. For many, this seems like an opportunity to party and spend money on products that constantly seek your attention.

In India, we say, the Goddess of money, Laxmi is flighty. It runs away in the blink of an eye. Before your money does that, invest. Do not be impulsive about spending your money.

The first-ever functional electronic TV was invented by the American inventor Philo T.Farnsworth. He was born poor and lived in a log cabin in Beaver, Utah. While in school, he won prize money for a magazine contest for inventing a magnetised car lock. Using that money he developed a tamper-proof lock and won a national competition, getting enough money to start a project of building an electronic appliance, while he was still in school. When his father died, the school student had to work on multiple jobs to support his family of four siblings. The idea of TV started nurturing in his mind when he was still in school.

Whatever extra money Philo earned went into buying tools and equipment to build something new. George Everson and Leslie Gorrel offered Philo a job in their bulk mailing business. The two employers were impressed at the dream Philo was nurturing and noticed that all his spare time and money went into his experiments. He explained to them the concept he was working on; the idea was to break down an image into parallel lines to project them on a screen for people to see. They agreed to fund the project, a new company named Everson, Farnsworth, and Gorrell was incorporated.

Philo worked hard in his lab and could finally send the first human image from a camera to the screen in the next room. In 1931 Philo joined Philco Radio Company, which provided him the research facility. He started getting invitations from companies and universities for helping them with various research. He left the full-time job to start his own company, Farnsworth Television and Radio Corporation. He invested every penny he earned beyond his necessities in research. He rolled out his TV sets, which were eventually approved by the US government, and he began to be known as the Father of Electronic Television. He obtained the patent for the TV.

He continued to invest his money in research, inventing many products. He worked long hours in his lab, which he called the 'cave'. He invented warning signals for defence, radar equipment, submarine detection devices, and an infrared telescope. He invested in the PPI projector for use of the air traffic control system. In 1999 he was mentioned in Time magazine's 'The Most Important People of the Century" list.

Chapter 12 Bargain Hunting

As a student of economics, I found it hard to digest why the same product is available at different prices at different stores. The hard fact is that if you do some research, you may find great bargains. Before you click the 'Buy' button, search other websites for the same product, it will surprise you to find how much discount you could get in some places. Bargains are everywhere. Keep your eyes and ears open. Companies offer a hefty discount during the end of season sale. In India during rains, before the start of Navratre, you could find great deals. Learn to time your purchases when there are discounts in the market. Always compare online and offline prices. Research to find out a cheaper product of another brand with the same specifications. Look for coupons wherever you can get them. Do you know why companies offer coupons instead of a straight discount? The surprising reason is that a few people use coupons and they lapse without being redeemed. When you are shopping on an on-line App, you are often offered a discount if you use a particular coupon code. The trick is that at the check-out window, the coupon code is not pre-filled but needs to be filled in from the memory. Not many people take the trouble of scrolling back to the window where the coupon code was written, and you lose the discount.

In the era of fast-changing technology, you will find new products being introduced at a considerable discount as the launch offer. Be on the lookout for those products.

Buy wholesale if you can consume a higher quantity. However, if you cannot consume the higher quantity, or do not have storage, this may not work for you. If you buy a 10 kg box of grapes instead of 1 kg that is your ideal quantity, you may not have space to refrigerate the extra stock and may end up wasting more money.

In certain markets haggling is the norm. Learn the fine art of bargaining at such places. It is fun, I can assure you. The vendor also appreciates a wise customer.

As a game, you can record how much you have saved monthly by hunting for bargains. You will be astonished to see how much you can save. A penny saved is a penny earned, if you invest that saved penny wisely.

Never consider the price tag (especially on big value items) as final. There is usually a scope for negotiation. Bargaining may make you look rude and uncouth, it may make you look cheap sometimes. Still don't be ashamed to ask for a lower price. The stress of asking for a price rebate will be more than upset by the discount you earn.

When buying high ticket things, do you research well before you walk into a showroom. Let the salesman know that you might not buy unless the specifications and the price are acceptable to you. Don't stick to one particular model, evaluate alternatives. Be prepared to walk out of the showroom if you do not get the right deal. You may give your contact details and ask the salesman to get back to you if he can improve the offer. You will be surprised to find that more often than not the price is negotiable. The shrewd buyer steals a bargain.

Develop a 'saver' mindset, as opposed to a 'spender' mindset. Some people get a kick out of spending. The more they spend, the more they enjoy it. Until they go broke. Become a reverse 'shopaholic'. Derive pleasure in saving rather than buying.

You like to buy things to keep up with your neighbours and peers. In economics, we call this the 'Demonstration Effect'. If you find a new BMW parked in your neighbour's garage, you will be tempted to buy one too. Get over these tendencies. Each person's spending habits and purchase decisions are their own. Do not let that be your guide. Learn to have utility and not the fad value as the criteria for buying things.

When buying grocery and daily needs stuff from the supermarkets, look for private labels. Let me share a secret here: the private labels- which means products packed and sold by the store's brand, like DMart and Big Bazaar- are usually produced by the same company and in the same factory that makes other brands. To cut costs by eliminating a chain of third-party producers and distributors, the store markets the products in its brand name. It may chop off as much as 25% of the price.

As far as possible, bring your lunch to the office. It will not only save you a lot of money but will also protect your health from the mass-produced restaurant junk which often includes sodium, trans-fats, sugar, and other bad elements beyond the permissible limits.

Think before you open the next pack of Haldiram's Classic coated peanuts or dig into a regular Non-Veg Supreme Pizza from Domino's. Only 35 grams of the scrumptious nuts would finish up around 35 percent of your daily permissible salt intake and 26 percent of the allowed fat consumption. And four slices of that cheesy pizza would make you consume 99.9 percent of the day's allowed salt and 72.8 percent of fats.

Eat one Chicken Maharaja Mac and your daily permissible salt intake is almost over in one go. It has 4.6 gm salt, leaving only 10 percent, or 0.4 gm more for the entire day. The fat content is over half the prescribed daily limit for a meal.

A medium McDonald's fries account for almost one-fifth of the daily fat need. The combo has an astounding 103 percent salt, 72 percent fat, 13 percent trans fat, and 33 percent carbohydrate.

Consumption of these junk foods, that are high in salt, fats, and trans fats can have deadly impacts. They are an open invitation to lifestyle diseases like diabetes, hypertension, heart ailments, and even cancer. Eating home-cooked food will save you not only in terms of direct money savings, but will also be a big saving in terms of the benefits accruing out of better health and lower obesity.

Traditional Indian food is nutritious and wholesome. Diet experts in the West now recognise this. Sticking to home-cooked food will save you big money both in terms of direct cost and the healthcare cost.

Replace your electric bulbs and lights with the power saving lED lights. Remember to turn off the lights and devices when not in use. Keeping your A/C at 25 or 26 deg Celsius will mean a great saving in terms of electricity bills. Do a cost-benefit analysis of using solar electricity. In India we are blessed with ample sunlight throughout the year. Solar energy is a pollution-free alternative to fossil-fuel electricity. While you will save on electricity bills, you will also do a favour to the environment.

Learn how to repair things. You can carry many of the minor repairs on if you have an inclination. It not only saves you money, but it also gives you a sense of fulfilment in being able to fix the things yourself.

Withdraw money from your own bank ATM. If you use the other bank's ATM's you could be charged extra bank charges. Read fine-prints, the less the transaction fees you pay in banking and in using cards, the smarter you are.

Buy e-books. They save on space and paper and cost less. I love reading paper books and keeping them as prized possessions. I use Francis Bacon's criteria to decide on which book to buy in paper form and which one on my Kindle. Bacon says, "Some books are to be tasted, others to be swallowed, and some few to be chewed and digested; that is, some books are to be read-only in parts; others to be read, but not curiously; and some few are to be read wholly, and with diligence and attention." If a book is important for me to be read again or for reference in the future, I buy a hard copy. All other books sit in my Kindle silently consuming no space. To a voracious reader who reads one book a week, this has meant a great saving.

Cars and other material possessions lose their value a day after we buy them. Your excitement in owning them is over in a couple of days. Most important, nobody in the world cares for what car you own. Even if they did, it should not be your concern.

Do not be lured by brands. You should not compromise on quality, but brands are not necessarily about quality. Often brands are built with millions of dollars of marketing and advertisement expenditure. The company must recover the brand-building cost from the customer by adding an overhead to the price. They continue to charge the premium even after the overheads have been fully recovered.

If you are clear of the specifications, and will do the research, you may buy the same product at a lower price without compromising on the quality. This is true in most cases, however, for inexpensive things you may have to decide if it is worthwhile in terms of time spent researching. For expensive things, gadgets, equipment, cars, and apartments, research is likely to save a lot of money for you. Developing an attitude of questioning the brand premium can give a great insight into the marketing strategy.

Fashion designers and retailers are constantly working to tempt you to buy. Don't do it. Change of fashion is a deliberate intervention by designers and brands to make you buy new clothes before the old one wears out. Gucci, Armani, Jaguar, Lamborghini being mentioned in Punjabi songs is a marketing trick.

True fashion, as defined by what people wear, changes slowly. The classics never go out of style. People keep accumulating accessories all their life and seldom wear them. Accessories last long, buy only when you need them.

The most important principle to learn is that whatever be your station in life, there will be people who live a better lifestyle than you. Unless you are the richest man in the world. Speaking of the richest men in the world, you will be astounded to see the life of simplicity that most of them live. Those who seem to live a life of luxury are also living way below their means. Their cost of living is a small fraction of their wealth. Another way of explaining this is that if their wealth were reduced to 10% of their present wealth, it still won't affect their living style. Nor a 10 times increase in their wealth would.

The only goal you should pursue is to increase your wealth tomorrow compared to your wealth today, so you can meet your financial goals and fulfil your attainable dreams. Stop comparing yourself to others.

Chapter 13 Neither a Tightwad nor a Spendthrift Be

All the desires, motives, and aspirations of human beings are clubbed together and defined as 'wants' in economics. Want is a lack of satisfaction which is supposed to be fulfilled by consuming the goods or services which fulfil it. There are some wants like love, affection, a sense of belonging that money does not satisfy. Such wants are not part of a discussion of the present chapter; we are discussing only economic wants here.

The basic characteristic of wants is that they are unlimited. All your wants can never get satisfied. When you satisfy one want, another one crops up. No amount of wealth is enough to satisfy all your wants. The means to satisfy the wants are limited.

Different wants have a different intensity. Some wants become urgent at some point in time and must be satisfied immediately. Many wants are competitive; since not all wants can be satisfied, wants compete with each other to attract the limited resources available.

Some wants are complimentary. They come in the wake of other wants. The recurring want of petrol comes after you satisfy your want of buying a car. Over time wants become habits difficult to break. Wants have the dangerous characteristic of becoming a part of your standard of living.

Traditionally we classify our wants as necessities, comforts, and luxuries. This classification seems to be fallacious. What is a necessity, comfort, or luxury for you is entirely in your mind. To a student addicted to on-line gaming, spending money on games looks like something he cannot live without. It acquires the definition of necessity. To an ascetic living on the mountains, food beyond a handful of wild berries and fruits seems a luxury.

Wants drive our economies. How much people want and what products people want determine the level and type of activities in the economy. Wants generate economic activities designed to satisfy those wants, this results in the creation of wealth for the producers, and satisfaction for the consumers, the resultant wealth generation leads to more want fulfilment, and the wheel keeps moving.

Clarity about your wants is a determinant of your wealth creation. Those who learn to live within their means have inculcated the ability to adapt according to the circumstances. I have come across people who are as happy riding the overloaded state transport bus as they are flying business class. They happily adjust to all material conditions. On the other end of the spectrum are the people who feel that to be seen in a casual dining restaurant, or economy class, or a low-priced shop would affect their ratings in the eyes of their friends. These people are all the time conscious of what others are thinking of them. Even if they have no money in their pockets, they must still spend.

There is a third category which I respect a lot. Warren Buffett, the third richest man in the world, lives a frugal life. He still lives in the house he bought in 1950, and drives a modest car. It is not unusual for him to hold his business meetings in Starbucks cafe. The chairman of Wipro Azim Premji is one of the richest men in India with a net worth of US$7.2 billion. He built his father's vegetable oil company into a global software empire with operations in dozens of countries, yet he still flies economy class. He walks to work. He does not own a yacht. Recently, he was responsible for the largest lump-sum donation in his country's history, pledging US$2-billion to support rural schools in India.

Whenever you spend your money, remember that you are saving it for the fund that will grow many times over your lifetime if invested instead of spending that money. Your savings have to be at the top of your list. Spending should be down on the list. You are the only person who can understand where you need to spend your money and how much. Not your spendthrift neighbour.

Be very careful of recurring expenses. Recurring expenses are like slow poison. Always be careful of them. Have you realised why

Apple wants to store your credit card details in your profile? So that it can automatically renew your monthly subscription to the online apps and games and music that you have subscribed to. The amount per transaction may be so insignificant that you cannot notice the text message you get from your bank (Some banks may not send an alert if the amount is less than Rs 5000) The cumulative effect of all the recurring transactions could be huge. You may not even know that there are some services you are subscribed to.

Your mobile phone company may entice you to 'Press 3' to make a particular ring tone yours. If you do that, you are subscribed to the service forever, and you will not easily discover that a hidden charge of a few rupees per month is being levied in your account month after month. Getting rid of such hidden subscriptions is one hell of a job.

Be very careful when you sign the ECS to your bank to authorise a third party to debit the bill amount directly from your account. I had a telephone connection from BSNL. After I instructed them to discontinue the service, they continued to debit the rental from my account for 2 years after disconnection. The bank refused to stop it; it said the mandate to discontinue should come from BSNL. Fighting with the government to get things done is a Herculean task.

The other end of the spectrum: People who spend too little

The frugal habits of some billionaires might surprise you. Mark Zuckerberg drives a $30,000 car, though he can afford to buy one Ferrari every month. Warren Buffett still lives in the same home he bought for $31,500 in 1958, though he can own islands. Bill Gates wears a $10 watch, and loves to wash his dishes every night, says it is therapeutic. Charlie Ergen, founder, and chairman of Dish Network still packs a brown-bag lunch from home every day eating out is expensive, and nothing like home-cooked food. Carlos Slim Helú, Mexico's richest man, drives himself around town and to work every day. He buys clothes off the rack at his retail stores. Walmart scion and a member of the richest family in America, Jim Walton works out of a plain old brick building in his hometown. He drives a rusting 15 years old Dodge Dakota pickup truck. John Caudwell, an English businessman and co-founder of mobile phone retailer Phones 4u, cuts his own hair. Amancio Ortega, the founder of Zara, eats lunch with employees in the Zara cafeteria. David Cheriton, the 'Professor Billionaire' who teaches at Stanford University, reuses tea-bags. Azim Premji, India's wealthiest tech tycoon, is said to monitor the number of toilet-paper rolls used by employees and always reminds employees to turn off the lights when leaving their offices. He often takes a cab from the Bangalore airport when returning home from business trips. He flies economy class and stays at company guest houses instead of five-star hotels. Vibha, the wife of Sun Pharma chairman Dilip Shanghvi occasionally commutes in Mumbai local market in an auto-rikshaw.

The Balance

Some people keep saving everything they have, accumulate enviable wealth, and die without enjoying the good things the money could have brought to them. There are people in California getting impressive paycheques who save almost everything they earn by sleeping in their car and eating at cheap fast-food joints. They may on their way to becoming millionaires. But is that life worth living? Money is a means to the fulfilment of your dreams, it makes life better; it helps you to do good to society. If the sole purpose of your life becomes to hoard money, you will die on a pile of cash. Tomorrow that you are accumulating your money for, may never come. Even if it comes, you may not have good physical or mental health to enjoy the fruits. You may lose your accumulated money in a bank crash or economic turmoil. Worst, and this is not uncommon in India, you may find your siblings sucking each other's blood to get a larger share of your inheritance.

A billionaire who pinches penny may have a purpose. When Azim Premji travels by cab, he is spreading the message of cost consciousness among thousands of Wipro employees. These people have reached the top of their actualisation pyramid. Though frugal about spending money on their own self, most of them have committed a large part of their wealth to philanthropy. They have made it big and they are now living for others. They are the Mahatma Gandhi of the 21st century.

But a lesser mortal must find a balance between the present and the future. We must curb the impulse to spend everything, and save a portion of our income, so it grows and we can live a more fulfilling life in the future. This balance between the present and the future is the key. Know when to stop spending, equally important to know where to stop saving. Neither a tightwad nor a spendthrift be.

The balance between saving and spending is akin to eating. Eat more and you risk getting obesity and other lifestyle diseases like diabetes; eat less and your body may starve of nutrition and may become deficient in essential micro-nutrients, and in some extreme cases it may lead to anorexia and death. In Indian cultural tradition, we consider food sacred, all religious traditions exhort you to eat in moderation. Respect money as well. Treat it as a resource to be judiciously used to satisfy your present and future needs. It is not to be squandered away.

People who've simplified their lives are happier than main-streamers. They are less materialistic, less status-conscious, more interested in personal growth, friends, family, and taking part in the life of their community. Happiness studies confirm again and again that these are the elements of a fulfilling existence.

Minimalistic Lifestyle:

Minimalism is all about living with less. This includes less financial burdens such as debt and unnecessary expenses. The philosophy is about getting rid of excess stuff and living life based on experiences rather than worldly possessions. You can probably see how having less stuff can also free up your life financially. Minimalism is the intentional promotion of the things we most value and the removal of anything that distracts us from it.

Here are some suggestions on minimalism:

1. Evaluate your space and examine your priorities.
2. Declutter every area of your home.
3. Store the things you can't part with.
4. Think before you buy new things.
5. Seek high-quality durable stuff.
6. Be grateful for what you have.
7. Regularly evaluate your stuff to see what has become a burden or unwelcome distraction in your life.
8. Disassociate from your material belongings.

Chapter 14 Stay Away From Scams

A fool and his money are soon parted. There are hundreds of cheats and scammers out there looking for gullible people luring them with attractive returns on their investments. The formula is the same since the Biblical times: double your gold, double your money in no time. People fall into the trap every day. Many people come to me after losing the money and admit that they fell for it because the return was too tempting. Unfortunately, they attempt to close the stable door after the horses have bolted. Remember, if it seems too good to be true, it probably is.

The first principle you need to learn is to protect your capital. You are to build your wealth on top of the capital that you painstakingly accumulate. If you lose it, you have lost the base. Keep in mind that there are no get-rich-quick schemes that work. Even if there were some, this book is not about them. I am interested in teaching you how to make wealth the slow and sure way.

We come across hundreds of examples of cheating every day all over the world. Some people never learn from their mistakes and get cheated repeatedly, some learn it the hard way after losing a fortune. New folks keep joining the crowd of gullible people waiting to be cheated.

Gold Sukh: Promoters of a little-known company in Jaipur promised 27 times return to investors in 18 months, mopped up over Rs 200 crore, and then made off with the money, leaving close to 200,000 people in the lurch. The company, Gold Sukh, was a multi-level marketing (MLM) company that told investors that their money would be invested in gold. More than the business model, investors were lured by the promise of stellar returns. It does not require a genius to figure out that this was a fraud. 27 times in 18 months! If a company made that kind of profit from its business, it does not need the investors' money, they can create wealth out of nothing.

A simple calculation shows that you need an 800 percent annual return to grow your investment 27 times in 18 months. The price of gold, in which the company was supposed to invest, has grown at an annual average rate of 23.5 percent in the past five years. At the present average bank fixed deposit rate of 6 percent, your investment will take over 56 years to grow 27 times. If you are getting a return worth 56 years in 18 months, it needs nothing more than an average IQ to figure out that this is a scam. Still, the scammers found 100,000 people who succumbed and lost Rs. 200 crores. Interestingly, the people who fall for such schemes are often the educated and enlightened segment of society.

This is not an isolated example. Every day a new scam is born, most of them are old wine packaged as new. People hoard their hard-earned money to hand over to them. When the culprit closes the shop, a new scam shop opens next door. When the devil closes one door, he opens another.

Then there was Speak Asia, a Singapore-based company that promised a Rs 4,000 monthly payout on an investment of Rs 11,000. The company claimed it did on-line surveys for big companies such as ICICI Bank and State Bank of India. It collected Rs 2,500 crore in less than two years before the authorities nabbed the company brass in India. I do not blame the criminals who float such companies(the world has its share of bad people), the blame must lie on the investors who do not see through the design.

These schemes are called Ponzi schemes. A Ponzi scheme is an investment fraud in which clients are promised a large profit at little to no risk. Companies that engage in a Ponzi scheme focus all of their energy on attracting new clients to make investments.

This new income is used to pay original investors their returns, marked as a profit from a legitimate transaction. Ponzi schemes rely on a constant flow of new investments to continue to provide returns to older investors. When this flow runs out, the scheme falls apart.

While they may be packaged differently, most Ponzi schemes have the following characteristics:

1.   A guaranteed promise of high returns with little risk
2.   A consistent flow of returns regardless of market conditions
3.   Investments that have not been registered with the government regulatory authorities
4.   Investment strategies that are secret or described as too complex to explain
5.   The clients are not allowed to view official paperwork for their investment
6.   The clients face difficulties in redeeming their money

Some Ponzi schemes operate under the garb of Multi-Level Market (MLM) companies, who pretend to be selling products and passing on a hefty commission to the down line. The real purpose is not to sell the product but to enrol more members who will pay more money to be paid to the up line and the promoters. In short, it is about finding more and more fools, until the last fools have been listed in the scheme, after which the scheme crashes. Some MLM companies are well-known names in the industry and are doing what looks like a legit business. My advice: say no to MLM.

The earlier in your career you understand protecting your capital, the better it will be for you. Return is proportionate to the risk, if an investment offers an exorbitant return, consider it as the first sign of a fraud brewing up. It is possible to get a higher than normal return in equities, but that requires a consistent approach and a deep study.

When you receive an investment proposal look at certain parameters. Ask for proper regulatory approvals. Fake companies flaunt unimportant registration numbers, like the number on the Registrar of Companies certificate, or sometimes fake registration numbers. Verify the credentials of the company you are investing in before you give them any money. If the agent asks you to issue cheques in the name of a third person, other than the company you are investing in, beware. Monitor your investment and ask for a regular account statement.

There is no such thing as easy money. Do not let greed blind your judgement.

Say no to Multi-Level Marketing

If you find a friend who is a "Business Associate" of Amway or Herbalife or Modicare or Oriflam, run!

MLM companies are now hidden everywhere. From multivitamins to beauty products to leggings, your friends are selling everything.

You probably know how it starts. You get a phone call from a friend (These days it also starts with a friend request on Facebook) whom you haven't met since school days, who wants to meet you and revive the wonderful bonds of friendship that you always had with her. She tells you she has a great business idea to discuss with you. If you ask her what the idea is, she says she will discuss it when you meet. Perhaps the idea is too precious to be disclosed on the phone. The friend turns up for a cup of tea and asks you if you would like to join a group of like-minded, ambitious people for a business where you can make huge profits by investing just a few thousand rupees. She then shows on her mobile phone the pictures of cheques of a couple of lakhs and a few thousand written by the MLM company in favour of its key associates. "People are making millions, they have left the day job and are working full time for it.", she says. Somebody who does not say no to friends is trapped.

MLM also called pyramid selling or network marketing is a marketing strategy for the sale of products or services where the revenue of the MLM company is derived from a non-salaried workforce selling the company's products/services, while the earnings of the participants are derived from a pyramid-shaped or binary compensation commission system.

MLM salespeople are expected to sell products directly to end-user retail consumers through relationship referrals and word-of-mouth marketing, but most importantly they are incentivised to recruit others to join the company's distribution chain as fellow salespeople so that these can become down line distributors. A salesperson earns income on the direct sales made by him and also gets a share from the sales made by his down-line. Theoretically, this looks great, however, 99% of people in any MLM lose money.

A friend, a salesperson from a top MLM company spent half an hour trying to convince me of the superiority of their toothpaste over the world's largest selling brand that I use. "Can't you pay a little extra for your health which is more important than all the money that you have?" For a moment I thought of giving in and buy a pack of toothpaste to get rid of him. On second thought, I realised that this toothpaste deal was a foot-in-the-door technique. I politely said no. I later discovered that nobody, especially the people who are in MLM don't mind your saying no. They are used to it, and they know that if they mind, they will lose another friend. Now when he meets me he seldom discusses MLM, he knows I am not a client material.

My advice for you: learn to say no when you find someone approaches you with a lucrative business proposal, doesn't require much investment and may make you a millionaire. If you cannot say no to that friend, run when you see them.

Chapter 15 Do I Really Need This?

It does not matter if a product or service is selling at a bargain price. The relevant question to ask is: do I really need it?

If you don't need a product, you don't have to buy it. Whatever be the price and whatever be the discount. Some people will buy even elephants if offered at a discount or in easy instalments. Learn to curb the impulse. The value of a product is not important, the value of that product to you is important.

Do not upgrade just because the company has announced a new model, and you must be seen carrying the latest one. Experience shows that usually there is just a cosmetic improvement between version 3.2 and version 3.3; and the improvement between version 3 and version 4 is also not too big to warrant an upgrade. My experience shows that you can survive a couple of versions before you need to change. Regarding some products and services version change may be significant but may not be useful to you, you can still survive with the old version.

One hint: Ignore ads from Amazon, Flipkart, Aliexpress, and others that pop up when you surf social media.

Warren Buffett, one of the richest men in the world, and the owner of 5.6% shares in Apple used to flaunt till recently his old-fashioned Samsung SCH-U320 phone bought many years back, till it broke down and he moved to an iPhone. He used to joke that Alexander Graham Bell gifted it to him. He could afford the most expensive diamond-studded phone in the world-Falcon Supernova iPhone Pink Diamond worth $48.5 Million still he was happy with the phone that you might be ashamed to show.

Maintain discipline. Know your needs. The sales and marketing team can extract every penny from your pocket. Your first big expenditure could be your car. The salesman will suggest lots of frills to boost your ego. Do you need that leather upholstery? And those big wheels? The sunroof? The difference in price between the mid-end and the top-end could be more than the extra utilities offered.

Buy the car that your current income level supports. The finance company may be happy to finance you based on your future income projections. My criteria is to be more conservative in calculating your future income than what the finance company does. As Indian road conditions and the quality of cars improve, you can easily run your car for 6-7 years without extra-ordinary maintenance. If you are one of those who think your car is your fashion statement or a success-certificate, understand that it is not. Since the car is an unproductive asset (it does not generate income) the longer you hold the existing car and delay the purchase of the new one, the more you gain in terms of protecting your wealth.

Till you can't afford to buy a new car, an old car is a good option. In India, two-wheelers are a cheap alternative to cars in the initial phase of your career.

When you buy the new car, like other gadgets it makes sense to buy the last year's model. Indian consumers are very fussy, and it takes one year to know how a car has fared. People buy cars when they are launched, lured by glamorous promotions, only to be dismayed after six months to find that nobody is buying that model now. Buy a tried and tested model which has been driving successfully for at least a year. You now only get value for money, you get a car with proven track records-literally.

Read your car User Manual cover to cover. Know when to change the oil. Know the right tyre pressure. If you maintain the right air pressure in tyres, it will save you a lot in terms of tyre wear and tear and the fuel mileage.

Drive your car until it drops.

Do not fill premium petrol/diesel in your car. I am sceptical of any additional benefits from the premium grade, even if there are, they are not worth the extra premium you pay.

Chapter 16 Pay Your Bills Promptly

If you do not pay your utility bill this month, the company will carry forward the amount to the next month, usually after adding a charge which is often higher than the market rate of interest. Even when no carry-over charges are levied, it is still good policy not to accumulate the bills, and pay them off promptly within the due date. It is about financial discipline and good habits. Have no debts and you will live happily.

This applies to all your government dues: municipal taxes, Income tax, GST, electricity bills, water bills. Pay them in time, and you will save lots of hassles later. If you forget to pay some government dues, or just procrastinate and forget later, the government may not remind you, it may seize your bank account. Every account is not Aadhar linked, your Income Tax PAN is everywhere, the Big Brother is watching you and you cannot escape. When you do not pay and the government comes to you to collect their dues, they may levy a heavy penalty. It may require intricate paperwork to get you out of the situation, the cost of which could be disproportionately higher than the amount you delayed. Make a rule in your life: No overdue payments, especially of the government.

Making prompt payment makes you a responsible citizen too. If we want our government to function properly, we as citizens must pay to the government its dues promptly.

If you feel the government has charged you something they should not have charged or has overcharged you, you may seek remedies available. However, always do a cost-benefit analysis in terms of time and money you will spend to win the argument. To illustrate, if you were to be charged Rs 500, and they have mistakenly charged you Rs. 520, you must weigh the efforts involved in reducing Rs 20 before litigating.

It is a good habit to check every bill you get. Few do that. There are instances of overcharging by mistake or sometimes charging the tariff under a wrong head leading to overcharging. If that is the case, it is not a one-off event, since the computer system will continue to charge an excessive amount until it is rectified. Spending 5 minutes extra on scrutinising your bills may prove to be a more fruitful hobby

Income Tax department wants you to pay tax on your income as you earn it. Known as 'Advance Tax' you are supposed to estimate the tax liability for the year in the first quarter, pay a portion of that, and fine-tune your calculations in the subsequent quarters as better figures become available to you. If you cannot pay the Advance Tax, you are required to pay high interest on the amount in default. Learn to calculate your tax liability and make sure you have paid all your dues during the year.

Sometimes you must spend more now so you can save more later. Make sure you are sufficiently covered for health insurance-something many Indians ignore. The high cost of medical treatment and hospitalisation may disrupt your life. Insurance takes the stress of such contingencies out of your life.

If you can prepay for your car maintenance, you usually save a lot. Cars often come bundled with free maintenance for 3-5 years at some premium. Opting for this may save you lots of hassles later. Cars demand little maintenance during the initial years, as they become old maintenance curve rises. It is sensible to pay a small premium initially to take care of the exorbitant future cost.

Similar deals are often possible in computers, air conditioners, and other equipment. It makes sense to pay AMC for expensive devices.

Chapter 17 Happiness is Being Debt Free

Debt is bad. Learn to live a debt-free life. Your bank will tell you debt is good. If your credit rating is good, they will disburse you loan without papers in a few minutes. If you don't want loans, they will send MBAs telling you how can you multiply your money by borrowing from them and investing (with them, sometimes). They are not in business to be your well-wishers. They make billions of Rupees out of interest from the money that people like you borrow. As I write this, an SMS just landed on my cell phone for the umpteenth time, looking into my credentials as a Chartered Accountant, a finance company wants to give me a pre-approved personal loan of Rs. 35 lakhs, at a ridiculously low rate of interest. Thank you, sir, for the honour, but I am not interested.

Don't fall into the trap. Debt may be good for the government, and sometimes for the corporations, but for an individual seeking to build your wealth, my advice is to stay away from debt as far as possible.

If you are in debt, get out of it at the earliest. To reiterate, stop spending before you earn, and don't spend more than you have. Avoid using credit cards, a debit card is a better option. Credit card company gives you interest-free payments until the next billing cycle, and you might think of this as a great idea to use other people's money without interest. They are smarter than you, and know that if allowed to spend beyond your means, you will not pay before the interest-free payment date. Beyond that date, you are charged with interest and hidden finance charges, the rate of which could be a shock to you. For the same reason, they want you to just pay 10% and carry over the transaction to the next billing cycle. So you can default again next month. My credit card company has never made a single rupee profit from me because I have never considered the credit card as a borrowing option, for me it is emergency cash, to be used in SOS situations. For them, I am not a good client. I have seldom used the card, have not done over 6 transactions in a year. The sales team often calls me to say that they are pleased to inform me they have given me a higher limit card which is being offered to but a few customers. I thank them for considering me worthy of that and graciously turn down the offer.

The credit card is like drugs. Learn to live within your means, no matter what. If you buy on a credit card, make it your priority to pay off the debt before the interest gets billed into your account. This has to be the priority, higher than any other priority.

Don't be fooled by the brownie points you get by spending more on credit cards. There is no such thing as a free lunch, the cookies were thrown at you are from out of the money collected from you.

If you want to make large purchases like a Europe trip, or an expensive iPhone, or a car, do not buy that on personal loan or credit card debt. Such loans are expensive, and the asset you purchase out of the loan is unproductive. It is not an asset but is an expense. A car depreciates the moment you drive it out of the showroom. Do proper research before you agree to the car loan. As a rule of thumb, remember that the longer the loan period, the higher will be the cumulative impact of interest per year. For other assets like iPhone and 80" TV ("fad purchases") it is unwise to take personal or consumer loans. Save first and buy after you have enough money to buy.

Chapter 18 The Time Value of Money

The time value of money means that a sum of Rs. 100 today is worth more than Rs.100 a year from now. It has still higher worth than Rs 100, two years from now. The longer the period, the higher is the value. This is because of the earning potential of money (and the inflation rate). To give a simple example, if the prevailing rate of interest is 6% pa, Rs 106 one year from now should be considered as equal to Rs 100 today.

The time value of money is based on the idea that people would rather have their money today than a later date. If you pay them on a later date, the amount that is due today, you must compensate for the period for which they will be deprived of their money through interest. If you hold someone's money for a longer period, you must also consider interest on the accumulated interest. This is known as compound interest.

The compound interest works magic in your favour. The longer the period of holding of your investment, the magic works better. However, let me warn you of a situation where this spiral may work against you and may destroy your wealth. When you take a loan with a long duration repayment period, the longer the period the higher is the interest you pay. For loans taken with a tenure of 7-10 years whatever EMI, you repay during the first few years of repayment shall go substantially towards interest. For instance, out of Rs. 100 you repay, as much as Rs 80 is likely to go towards interest, and it will reduce your principal by only Rs. 20. It is only around the middle of your tenure will the higher allocation goes towards the principal. This brings us to an important principle: think twice before you commit a long term loan. If you can't do without a loan (for example, when buying a house) study the repayment terms carefully. Read the fine prints. Do the terms and conditions permit you to prepay the loan? If they do, make sure that the terms read that the additional amount you pay will reduce your principal immediately, and shall not be kept as money in suspense. Banks are smart, they know, not many people read the loan documents. Read all documents before you sign the dotted line. It will save you a great deal of money.

The Rule of 72

The Rule of 72 is a wonderful mental aid to calculate the compound rate at which your investment or loan will double. It almost works like magic. While you can always calculate the exact rate by doing mathematical calculations or by using a spreadsheet, this simple formula is handy for quick decision making. The rule is simple, divide the number 72 by the interest rate you are receiving, and you will find the number of years it will take to double your money.

The Rule of 72 is said to have been invented by one of the greatest scientists of all times Albert Einstein who had said considered the compound interest to be the most popular force on earth. He said, "...compound interest the eighth wonder of the world and mankind's greatest invention because it is the mightiest force ever unleashed for the amassing of wealth".

Some examples:

At 6% interest, your money takes 72/6 or 12 years to double.

To double your money in 10 years, get an interest rate of 72/10 or 7.2%.

If your country's GDP grows at 5% a year, the economy doubles in 72/5 or 15 years.

If the growth slips to 3%, it will double in 72/3 or 24 years. If growth increases to 7%, the economy doubles in 72/7 or 10 years.

Chapter 19 Money Matters

I made a quick search for "make money fast" on Amazon.com. It returned over 2,00,000 results. Go through any of those 2,00,000 books each one would give a magic formula that may make you a millionaire, with little efforts. Just follow the formula, and money will keep pouring in. I wish life was that simple.

If you are looking for making money fast, this book is not for you. This book is not for people in a hurry. It is for people willing to learn the principles they can apply and make their investment grow by taking advantage of market idiosyncrasies and the power of compounding. This book is for those who will understand investing as a life-time pursuit, which will help them realise their dreams, and create a stable source of income and wealth.

I did not search that on Google, for I can imagine, if over 2,00,000 books talk about making money fast, how many websites and blogs must talk about them. In the world of big data analytics and information overload, so much information is available to us by the click of the mouse, or a touch of the screen (or sometimes, "Hey Siri, can you tell me....") that it becomes impossible to sift the usable knowledge out of the heap of incongruous data. One thing that has not improved in the on-line real-time era is common sense. It continues to be uncommon and in some ways has diminished. It seems to lose out as people gain more and more of technical skills, but do not understand and appreciate the larger picture.

There are some equipped with common sense, the insight to think, and that trait is common to all successful investors. Contrary to what many of us would believe, you need not be an Ivy League graduate with a degree in finance and economics to attain Financial Independence.

Warren Buffett has always maintained that IQ is not the single defining factor in investment success. *"You don't need to be a rocket scientist. Investing is not a game where the guy with the 160 IQ beats the guy with a 130 IQ. Rationality is essential.",* says Buffett. Even if you have an IQ of 160, Buffett says you should just "give away 30 points to somebody else" because "you don't need a lot of brains to be in this business."What you do need is emotional stability," he adds."You have to be able to think independently."

Charlie Munger says, *"It is remarkable how much long-term advantage people like us have gotten by trying to be consistently not stupid, instead of trying to be very intelligent. There must be some wisdom in the folk saying: 'It's the strong swimmers who drown.'"*Strong swimmers often get into trouble by swimming into deeper waters. Weak swimmers stay close to the shore. We are not interested in complicated mathematical equations that are designed to exploit short term windows in the market to make quick money.

Money is abstract and indifferent

You cannot touch money. It is abstract. You can touch a gold coin, or a Rs 100 note. The gold coin is a metal, and the currency note, a piece of paper-A piece of paper that gives you a right to meet a Rs 100 worth of obligation.

Money is neither good nor bad. It is the craving for money that could be good or bad. Money is indifferent to what or who you are. It doesn't care for your race, ethnicity, sex or the colour of your skin. It makes no difference to money if you are a criminal or a sage. Money treats you all equally. It is not biased, if you are a billionaire or a poor person, money does not pass any value judgement, it does not care if you are worthy of owning it or not.

Money is important

Whoever said money can't buy happiness didn't know where to go shopping. To quote W. Somerset Maugham, "Perhaps the most important use of money - It saves time. Life is so short, and there's so much to do, one can't afford to waste a minute; and just think how much you waste, for instance, in walking from place to place instead of going by bus and in going by bus instead of by taxi."

Money is not a bad thing. Capitalism has earned a bad name because of the abuse of money some people do. Money earned ethically is not bad at all, and you can do incredible things with it. You can use the money to make the world a better place, you can use the money to improve the quality of life of the people around you. Money in the hands of honest people is a blessing to the world. Make more money, help your family enjoy a better lifestyle, help people around you, help the world. Do everything you can to ease the world of its miseries.

Money is not everything, but money can solve many problems. You are stressed up because of unpaid bills, the solution to the stress is money. For the health of your ageing parents, the solution is money. Education of your children, the solution lies in money. When worrying about the money is off your table, you can do better things in life.

Stop believing that money is evil. Ill-gotten wealth is, money in the hands of evil people is evil. Bill Gates has committed 45% of his wealth to charity. That amounts to US$41 billion. The money goes towards health and education in the underdeveloped world. You may wonder why he made so much money that he ultimately gives away.

Creation of wealth is easier than you think

Every year thousands of people join the millionaire and the billionaire club. If you look into their background, few of them were born with a silver spoon. Some of them were lucky: their rich uncle kicked the bucket, leaving no other legal heir. Some won a lottery. But a large majority of them worked their way up.

The subject of this book is the people who used proven ways to create wealth and reaped success. This book picks up the distilled information from the lives of successful investors and presents it in a ready-to-use format.

We offer no abracadabra; the book is not about short-cuts; it is not about speculation and gambling. It does not promise to teach something that the author has discovered buried in a pot under the sea. It teaches the principles of success in wealth maximisation , principles are there in the public domain, principles which people like Warren Buffett have put into practice and made it big. Though not a magic, they work with magical precision if applied faithfully.

Money matters, money is important, but money is not everything

I have been speaking about the importance of money, and why you cannot do without money. That theme will run throughout the book. However, let it be clear in the beginning that money is not the be-all-and-end-all. There is a limitation to things money can do. It can take you some distance, but not too far.

If money were everything, you would not have unhappy rich people. Many land in depression and many commit suicide not because they run out of money, but because they are unhappy. Unhappiness could stem from hundreds of real or perceived reasons.

There are things money cannot buy. They include respect, love, trust, manners, conscience, integrity, intelligence, common sense, peace of mind, patience. All these traits are earned out of hard work, sincerity, and dedication over time. Any attempt to buy them with money may prove counterproductive.

Health is more important than money. Health is the necessary condition while money is a sufficient condition. We need both of them, to live happily. But as you can see, the necessary condition is always more important.

A certain fact is that we can't buy health with money. Today, there are still some diseases that have no cure. Wealth doesn't always make life more healthy and happy. If you are a billionaire, you always feel unsafe. Afraid of being killed or kidnapped for your fortune will speedily harm your health and shorten your longevity.

Furthermore, without being fit, how can you enjoy your wealth. If a man has wealth, he can have everything. As an old saying goes: Where there is health, there is life .

Money without good health is not worthwhile.

Finally, the most important thing is your family. No amount of money is a substitute for a happy family.

You cannot take money with you when you die. These last words of a billionaire might resonate in your ears for quite some time: "In other eyes, my life is the essence of success, but aside from work, I have a little joy, and in the end wealth is just a fact of life to which I am accustomed.

At this moment, lying on the bed, sick, and remembering all my life, I realise that all my recognition and wealth that I have is meaningless in the face of imminent death.

You can hire someone to drive a car for you, make money for you - but you can not rent someone to carry the disease for you. One can find material things, but there is one thing that can not be found when it is lost - 'life'."

"Wealth is like health: Although its absence can breed misery, having it is no guarantee of happiness," says psychology professor Dr. David G. Myers.

Chapter 20 Some Rules for Financial Independence

Multiply by 25 (x25)

I am often asked by my clients to define how much savings they should accumulate to retire comfortably. I use the commonsense method, an effective rule of thumb, to determine the amount of capital to be accumulated. Estimate the amount you need as your future annual expenditure, multiply that by 25, the resulting figure is the amount of corpus you must create for your Financial Independence. For example, if your estimated expenditure is Rs 12 lakhs per annum, you must have 12,00,000X25= Rs 3 crore. To some of you, this may look like a conservative figure, since the rate of interest in India, and the normal return on equities and other investment classes in India is likely to be higher; yet I will prefer to make a conservative estimate. The rule considers an annual rate of return of 4%, if you are a disciplined equity investor your annual return can be from 10 to 14%, in which case, you can accumulate the desired amount faster. Thus, you may consider 'multiply by 25' to be a basic formula that should work for all, though for some people the multiplier could be around 20. This makes your investment inflation-proof, and it can also withstand the impact of calamities like a financial crisis and COVID-19.

The credibility of calculations depends upon how accurately you can estimate the future desirable income level. If you are likely to get some pension or some passive income like rent or royalty, you may reduce that while calculating the corpus.

4% Rule

You are likely to confuse between the 4% rule and the x25 rule because x25 also factors in a 4% discount rate. However, both rules serve different purposes. While you use x25 to calculate the amount of savings you should accumulate to attain Financial Independence, 4% rule is about how much money you should withdraw from your account, once you live on your savings. 4% rule is thus a rule for post-retirement. You need not worry about it during the time you are accumulating your savings.

According to this rule, once you stop working you should not withdraw over 4% from your savings every year. Given that the Indian economy grows faster than the world economy, and that the real return on investment in India, net of inflation, is likely to be higher than 4%. 4% is thus a conservative withdrawal, which will also take care of change in the valuation of your investment arising out of erratic market fluctuations.

Thus, if you have Rs 2 crore in your investment account, you should not withdraw more than Rs. 8 lakh from your account annually if you want your investment to continue to grow to serve you during your entire lifetime. We have worked on this formula on an estimated life of 30 years post-retirement. If you estimate this period to be 20 years, you may withdraw a higher percent. However, if you want to survive on the accumulated savings for 40 years, the rate of withdrawal has to be less than 4%.

Becoming financially independent doesn't have to be about quitting your job. It's about having choices. If you love your work, by all means, keep working. Just that you don't have to carry the stress of where your next meal will come from. Once you are financially independent, you may choose not to work for money but passion.

Chapter 21 Online Shopping

Online shopping is a great thing. It has made buying easy, you can shop 24X7, you can browse through thousands of products before selecting the product you want to buy, you don't have to go out of your home to buy; it saves on petrol and driving time, you can send gifts to your friends anywhere in the world, and you have a wide range of products in stock to choose from that your local store may not carry.

However, remember the following guidelines before you buy online.

1. Appearances are deceptive. The actual look of the product may differ from what it seems in the picture. Professional photography is employed to create alluring images. If you have used a product before it may not be much of a problem buying it again. However, for a new product, read the specifications carefully, and do proper research. Carefully note the size of the product. With no frame of reference, the image may not give an idea of scale. Once I was fascinated by an artifact at an online seller and bought it. When it arrived, I was shocked to find that it was a miniature almost of the size that hangs on a key-chain. In the picture, it looked like a big statue!

2. Hidden cost: Look for the hidden costs before you order. Shipping costs may not be disclosed to you till you go to the payment option. Adding the shipping cost may make the product more expensive than that of competitors. Sometimes, GST is added at the payment stage. The psychology is to lure you into buying, and by the time you reach the payment window, you have already spent time on the site so even if expensive; you agree to go ahead. Or sometimes you don't notice that your payment total has increased by 18%. Air ticketing agents use another strategy, they show a cheap price. Once you fill in the details, the loading starts. First, the credit card/online banking processing charges, then frills with boxes checked already. If you are careful not to uncheck them, the amount gets added to the final bill.

Donation to charity, travel insurance, and many other items come in this category. Some companies charge a higher price for a particular colour. The colour you like will be the most expensive of the lot.

3. Overspending: Online shopping tempts you to overspend. Products are bundled together. When you buy one beauty product you get ads for a complementing product. Many platforms like Aliexpress offers a discount if you buy on mobile apps. On your desktop, you are usually sitting at your usual place and are in control of the situation. Research into competitive websites is also possible. You are less impulsive on a laptop or desktop.

You are encouraged to save your credit card number. They offer you brownie points if you do so. Once you store the number, you are also happy since it makes transactions smooth and quick. The real purpose behind this is to encash on your impulse. You find something good, and before you can think further, you have the option of one-click checkout which completes the transaction before you realise it. Remember, you are just one click away from a debt.

4. Return: While on some sites like Amazon returning is a pleasant experience, on most Indian sites returning is a pain. I have had my share of bad deals. One vendor wanted me to bear the return freight and send the parcel, and I was promised the freight would be reimbursed too. Courier charges may be high when an individual pays them, companies have a bulk deal pricing. Neither the freight nor the original amount came back. I had bought an expensive motorcycle riding jacket from a vendor on Amazon. Found it too tight. When I tried to return it, could not find the return option, called the vendor who asked me to read the terms and conditions specified at Amazon which said that if a buyer intended to return they must ship it at their own cost, and will also have to bear the shipping cost of the replacement.

5. Check for reviews: Product reviews by others can give you clues. Be careful of paid-reviews and fake-reviews by the vendor and

their people. Especially read the negative reviews. Some negative reviews may be by competitors. If you apply your mind properly, you may judge if the review is genuine or the intention behind the review is to entice or discourage you to buy.

6. Beware of cyber-crimes: Identity theft, credit card theft, and many other crimes are committed every day in the digital world. Do not buy from the platforms you do not trust. Fake sellers tempt you by offering cheap prices. If the price seems too good to be true, it probably is. The hidden intention could be to steal your personal information, or the product could be a fake or cheap imitation. Or it may be a product from an unauthorised seller who buys the product from the international market or grey market, the Indian division of the company may not honour the warranty on such products.

Chapter 22 Read Before You Sign

When you take a loan or buy insurance, the company hands you a 20-page contract- usually pre-printed- with smaller fonts than what your eyes can read. The manager sits on your head and wants you to sign the document, and once you do that, he congratulates you on becoming an esteemed customer of their company.

Few take the pain to read the documents they are signing. Make it a rule: do not sign any document without reading it and without understanding its meaning. If it takes time, take your time. The impatience of the other party to the contract should make you more cautious. You may tell them it is your principle to sign after reading. If the contract is intricate and technical, you may have to seek the help of a lawyer to understand it.

Not that all companies you deal with are out there to take you for a ride. But there could be some. Unless you understand the rights, liabilities, and obligations you are about to commit to, how can you agree to them? You are agreeing to something you are not even aware of. Until you are dragged in court for non-fulfillment of your obligation under the contract.

Do not treat a printed text as the scriptures. They must be amended if they differ from what you have agreed upon. If any changes are made, both parties should sign to accept the amendment.

After signing the contract, get a copy to be retained in your records. You have a right to a copy of the contract, insist that you want it when you sign it. Carefully file your copy at an appropriate place where you can retrieve it from when you need it.

Make no oral agreement on anything significant and material. As time lapses, memory fades. People interpret the terms based on their perception, based on faded memory. This may confuse and may lead to litigation. If the deal is of a significant amount, or involves intricacies, reduce the terms to writing. When in doubt, go back to the written document.

Consider having a proper filing and storage system to store your important documents. Have a secure and reliable backup of your digital documents. The question is not 'if' your hard disk will fail but 'when'. Cloud backup is a great option. Secure very important documents by backing them up at two places. The backup plan should be in place as an automatic measure. Regular data backups lead to peace of mind. In the event, a cyber-crime system crashes or disasters occur, there is a backup ready to go to recover.

Chapter 23 Bookkeeping

Be your accountant. Learn to record the transactions. Whatever be the area of your specialisation, it is this one skill you ought to have. Record keeping is easier than you think. It requires basic knowledge that can be acquired easily, and it requires conscious efforts and a habit to record every transaction. You can record them in a diary, or on a journal, cash-book and ledger, or a spreadsheet, or one of the many user-friendly accounting packages and apps available. Choose your mode, but record you must. Develop a habit of recording your receipts and payments daily. It will surprise you how useful this one habit can be.

Bookkeeping helps you budget your income and expenditure. Unless you record your transactions, you have no clue about where your money goes and most times where it comes from. Knowing your current receipts and payments is the first step towards budgeting for your future.

Bookkeeping gives you information for the preparation of your tax returns. As a CA firm, we scramble through a load of raw data clients bring to us every accounting season, deciphering that data is a real pain in the neck for us. There is always the risk of missing on some information or classifying some information under the wrong head. There are however a few clients who record their data meticulously and come to us with the detailed statements in the form required by us, brimming with confidence. Some people can plan their taxes better. They pay lower taxes using the legal route of tax-avoidance. There is a very thin dividing line between tax-avoidance and tax-evasion: the former is your right, the latter may land you in jail.

By definition, bookkeeping is the organisation of financial information. By organising your financial information, you are in control of your life. You have all the required inputs at your fingertips. You know how much vehicle insurance you paid last time and can compare it to the current premium. If the company tries to overcharge you, you have ready data to argue.

Disorganised books may weigh heavily on your mind. You do not remember how much you owe to others, or how much others owe to you. As a general rule, if you owe money to someone, eventually he will remind you to replay. (Efficiency demands that you pay off before it falls due, instead of waiting for reminders) However, nobody will ever remind you of the money others owe to you. (Unless they are rare exceptions who have read this book or follow the principles enumerated here, though haven't yet read this) If you lose track of that debt, it is gone. Bookkeeping gives you the peace of mind that comes from being systematic and organised.

Efficiency demands that you never bounce your cheques. A bounced cheque is not only bad on your reputation, but it also reflects poorly on your financials. It may also land you into a lawsuit. Banks levy exorbitant charges when you bounce a cheque. Never issue a cheque that you have not provided for.

The American billionaire Julian Robertson is spot on when he says, "Accounting was the course that helped me more than anything.". The billionaire Warren Buffett is known to maintain his accounts himself.

The first book on the modern double-entry bookkeeping that the world follows was written by a priest Luca Pacioli in 1494. While Friar Luca is regarded as the "Father of Accounting," he did not invent the system. Instead, he simply described a method used by merchants in Venice during the Italian Renaissance period. His system included most of the accounting cycle as we know it today. Can you believe nothing has changed in the fundamental accounting concepts for centuries? If a friar of the 15th century could write a book on the accounting system, you should know that it has to be a simple and easy-to-understand system. You do not have to be a CA or a commerce graduate to understand the accounting system. You just need the inclination.

Computers have taken over the accounting job with perfection. You need not know the fundamental accounting concepts to maintain your accounts. Still, the knowledge of accounting helps. You may do a summer course on the accounting concepts and also getting familiar with one of the popular accounting software. Modern accounting software like Tally and QuickBooks go beyond accounting and provide analytical inputs for management decision making.

Chapter 24 Spend time with yourself daily

One of my all-time favourite poems comes from the Welsh poet William Henry Davies:

What is this life if, full of care,
We have no time to stand and stare.
No time to stand beneath the boughs
And stare as long as sheep or cows.
No time to see, when woods we pass,
Where squirrels hide their nuts in grass.
No time to see, in broad daylight,
Streams full of stars, like skies at night.
No time to turn at Beauty's glance,
And watch her feet, how they can dance.
No time to wait till her mouth can
Enrich that smile her eyes began.
A poor life this if, full of care,
We have no time to stand and stare.

With mobile phones, laptops, and other gadgets constantly seeking our attention and tracking our progress, do we have time for ourselves? In a connected world, we need to disconnect often. Disconnect, so we can connect with ourselves. Disconnect so we can find time to smell the roses. Disconnect, so we can recharge our batteries. Disconnect, so we contemplate. Disconnect, so we can see the bigger picture. Disconnect, so we can mark our progress on our life's road-map.

To keep up with all the data flowing constantly on our screens, we do not get time for creativity. In the connected world, creativity is the first casualty. The first step towards creative thinking is to stop all the noise and clutter that devices create. Learn to schedule a disconnect. Whenever you think of productivity, you think of installing one more app, when you should uninstall an app or two.

There are many reasons to schedule a break with yourself and to simplify your digital life. Let us discuss some of them.

1. **Meta-cognition**: Meta-cognition is thinking about one's thinking. More precisely, it refers to the processes used to plan, monitor, and assess one's understanding and performance. Metacognition includes a critical awareness of a) one's thinking and learning and b) oneself as a thinker and learner.

Meta-cognitive practises increase students' abilities to transfer or adapt their learning to new contexts and tasks. Meta-cognitive practices help you realise their strengths and weaknesses as learners, writers, readers, test-takers, group members, etc. A key element is recognising the limitations of one's knowledge or ability and then figuring out how to expand that knowledge or extend the ability.

By spending time alone, we can reflect more, to think differently, and to think more creatively. The ability to reflect on our thoughts is to find new and fresh perspectives to seemingly stale ideas.

Keeping a journal can help. Write your thoughts daily. During your meta-cognition time, reflect on your thoughts, jot down things that come to your mind. Strive to make the ideas workable.

Reflecting on old problems, situations, and circumstances will help you understand the viewpoints of others, and provide insight and knowledge that you otherwise would not receive.

2. **Memory Improvement**: Do you wonder why do we close a meeting or a phone conversation with the summary of the action points? If you talk to someone for half an hour, and discuss lots of

action points, and conclude the call without summarising the discussion, the chances are that the actions will be either forgotten or confused. This is so because the brain organises the thoughts in the pause after the conversation is over. If that window is small, it will remember only some points and may not organise all thoughts.

Your memory enhancement needs a break from the clutter and noise. The more frequent are the pauses you take, the better is the memory-organization and improvement. Sleep is the biggest pause of the day, and while you might think of it as an impediment to the work-flow, it enhances productivity. When you are asleep, your brain is systematically filing the data in their rightful cabinets. Sleep experts recommend eight hours of sleep for optimum performance.

During sleep, you have no control over the process. What is recommended for further productivity enhancement is a pause where you are not asleep but are contemplating, in a complete one-to-one relationship with yourself, uninterrupted by any outside noise.

An afternoon nap helps improve your productivity dramatically. If your work style permits you to take a short nap in the afternoon, go for it. It will boost your memory, control your blood pressure, and calm your nerves, improve alertness, enhance creativity, and boost your willpower. If an afternoon nap is not an option, just quiet rest or meditation can do wonders. Simple breathing exercises can help slow down your brain and might be restorative.

You may like to call it meditation, contemplation, isolation, solitude, seclusion; the label does not matter. When I do my daily quota of running 10 km or riding 40 km, I use that time for spending with myself, with no distractions. While my legs run, my brain meditates.

3.   **Short 30 min holiday:** This break is like a super-quick holiday for you. This holiday rejuvenates you. You emerge fresh and energetic out of it. You should have a structured life, however, your

mini-breaks should be a part of the structure and not a departure from it. When you plan your day, find out what time of the day will you have the meeting with the most important person in your life: Yourself. For me, this break works better when I combine it with my workout session, but you can plan it your way. Maybe during your lunch break? Maybe combining a 10-minute nap with the 30-minute mini-break? Or when walking your dog? Or a part of your regular yoga session? Remember, this short break is a super-charger. Do not skip.

4. **It helps you stop negative influence at the door:** The pause helps you to absorb your day's work. It also helps you not to be swayed by the negative influence of some people around you. It helps you constantly monitor people not within your inner circle but seem to influence you. Introspection allows you to sift and weed out negative thoughts and negative influencers. If you do not disconnect yourself from society, you will not discover who you are, what are your unique strengths, and how are you progressing towards your goals.

So instead of watching a TV show, or listening to music, or reading a book, find a quiet time each day, where you are completely disconnected from the rest of the world, where you can introspect, imagine, visualise, and think creatively.

One word of caution: there is a thin line between withdrawing from the society to contemplate, and to become a recluse. As soon as your short journey into your mind is over, it is time for you to get back into the world. Be careful not to become an escapist. Do not let that time become a window for negativity to creep in. Do not leave society, engage in society differently.

Set yourself apart—strive to break habits, use your time in solitude to find out your unique perspectives, to engage in meta-cognition, to create stronger memories. It might surprise you to see a manifold enhancement in your creativity.

5. Mindful Meditation: Develop a practice focused on stilling the mind. One of the simplest forms of mindfulness meditation is to find a quiet place, sit comfortably on a chair or cushion, and set a timer for anywhere between five and 25 minutes. Then start observing the in and out of your breath. You might count the breath, starting with one on an in-breath, then two on an out-breath, going up to 10, and then returning to one. Whichever method you use, you're likely to notice the nearly constant stream of thoughts that run through our minds. Allow the mind to detach from these thoughts and to experience a sense of openness.

Do this regularly. The way consistency is the key to the physical exercise, you must meditate regularly for better effectiveness. You may combine your meditation session and the session on spending time with yourself, though both are diametrically opposite activities. Meditation requires you to block your brain completely of thoughts; spending time with yourself is disconnecting from the world and introspect. If you decide to combine the two sessions, be aware of this difference, and know when to switch over from the first to the second.

Chapter 25 How Much Cash to Keep for Emergency

I would not have written this chapter but for the worst tragedy that has just hit mankind. The pandemic has caused an unprecedented recession in history, and we will see the severest job cuts ever. Many companies may not survive the aftermath and may throw in the towel. Many will struggle to make both ends meet.

Though I always advise people to keep a contingency reserve of three to six months, the crisis demands that I spend more time explaining that.

Calamities may strike, sudden job loss may happen, lock-down may happen. Be prepared for the black-swan events. Keep funds in liquid or semi-liquid form for such situations.

I have stressed two points elsewhere in this book, which is relevant here. First, budget your income and expenditure. If you know how much money is likely to come to you and how the money will you need for meeting your expenses, you will have clarity about the corpus of an emergency fund. Second, you must record your income and expenditure. This is the record of transactions that have taken place.

If you lose your job, it may take about 3 months for you to take another job. If you are a self-employed professional dependent on a few clients, and you lose your key client, you may suddenly feel the cash crunch. If you are in business, and a force majeure event strikes, it may disrupt your business activities for a couple of months. You should have a sufficient amount in your bank account or near-liquid securities.

Should this money be lying in your bank account? The recent fallout of Yes Bank (It survived thanks to government intervention) and PMC Bank make us think of the possibility of failure of the banks. The solution lies in keeping your emergency funds in nationalised banks or gilt-edged or blue-chip securities. Diversification is the key here. Do not trust the whole of your emergency fund in one basket. Spread it out in a few asset-classes so that if one basket falls, you have 6 others to withdraw from.

Whether you should keep the amount in a low-interest-bearing savings account or any other form of investment will depend upon your ability to withstand crisis, and safety you desire, and the cash-churn time of your investment. I, for example, keep even my emergency fund in equities. This may be risky for most of the readers. In an economic crisis strikes, the first casualty is the securities market. However, my fund has grown considerably over the years I have invested it in equities, so even if I am required to make a distress sale, I will still spend out of a large profit I have already made over the life of my corpus. You may decide on how to keep your emergency fund tailored for your individual needs.

The money should be immediately accessible when you need it. When you have money lying in your emergency fund account, you have peace of mind. You know that if you fall sick, or meet with an accident, or the sky falls, you still have money to support yourself and your family. This feeling alone should put you at peace. However, if you do not have the fund, you will keep thinking of what happens when suddenly your flow of income stops. How will you pay the rent or the EMI of the car or house? This feeling affects your emotional and physical health. If you have no cushion, you will fear taking risks. You will stick to the present job, however mundane or low paying it may be. Because you are scared that if you lose your job, you have nothing else to fall back upon. As they say, "Scared money don't make money". Having no emergency makes your money scared money which makes no money.

Chapter 26 Healthy Mind, Healthy Body

Health is more important than anything else. When I discuss financial planning with my busy clients and enquire about what are they doing for keeping themselves healthy and fit, I often hear interesting excuses; the most common is that they don't get time for a workout. I then explain to them they need to invert the priority pyramid. The priority should be health- both physical and mental-everything else comes later.

You may not enjoy the fruits of money you save when the time comes because you may not be healthy enough to do so.

YOU are your priority. If you put yourself first, you are never too busy. Health is the foundation on which you build the edifice of your success. If the foundation crumbles, the whole structure comes falling.

A healthy lifestyle goes beyond just maintaining a healthy diet and activity levels, but also includes managing stress, sleep, and even the amount of information you consume each day.

Here are some things you must do to maintain a healthy lifestyle.

1. Make a daily schedule. List what kind of workout you will do each day. Allocate time for the workout. In case, something causes you to miss a workout- for example, a rain spoiling your morning run- have a backup plan ready.

2. Sleep well. Sleep is the most neglected priority. You must target eight hours of sleep daily. If you sleep less one day, you must try to make up for the lost one the next day. Do not deprive yourself of sleep for two or more consecutive days. While you are sleeping, your brain is not resting, contrary to popular belief. It is working overtime housekeeping and filing and organising the information. Your mind and body are repairing themselves of all damages the activities and stress have caused. Sleep heals, sleep cures. Sleep is not negotiable.

Digital screens cause high voltage disturbance in your brain. After you switch off your devices, it takes quite some time for your brain to unwind itself from the impact of high-resolution light. Switch off all digital devices at the earliest after dinner, so that brain takes you towards naturally induced sleep.

3. Drink a lot of water. The body is about 60% water. You are constantly losing water from your body, primarily via urine and sweat. To prevent dehydration, you need to drink adequate amounts of water. To function properly your body and brain need a regular supply of water, dehydration may affect your kidney and other organs, and may also affect the brain's functioning.

Stay sufficiently hydrated all the time. Individual requirements may vary and will depend on body composition, activity level, weather condition, and a host of other factors, however, drinking at least 2 litres of water a day is a minimum recommendation. My rule of thumb is to drink before you are thirsty; thirst is not the first, but the last response of your body. It is the body's defence mechanism. If you are thirsty, it is already late. In cold weather, your body may not respond with a thirst indicator, be more careful to drink water in winter.

Another test I use to determine if I am sufficiently hydrated is the pee test. The lighter the colour, the more hydrated you are. Dehydration is caused when the volume of water in the body is depleted. And when we are dehydrated, our kidneys, which filter waste, tell the body to retain water. Therefore, we have less water in our urine, which causes it to become more concentrated and darker.

4.   Eat a balanced nutritious diet. Include lots of veggies, fruits, and good protein sources. Use a full spectrum of colours found in vegetables and fruits. Learn to listen to the fullness indicator. Be careful of what you eat when you are exercising actively since you believe that an extra helping will not harm you as you are burning calories. The rate of calorie burn is slower than the number of calories that each extra bite contains. Avoid junk food at all costs. If you can

afford the luxury of home food, go overboard on that. You will never go wrong with the food cooked at home. Ration the intake of the white substances: sugar, flour (Maida), salt. Nourish your stomach with probiotic foods regularly. Herbs and spices in the Indian kitchen are a great source of micro-nutrients and antioxidants, use them liberally. Deep frying food cause carcinogens, avoid. For the same reason, avoid trans-fats.

Dieting is a short-term solution. Draw a long term sustainable eating pattern, a plan which does not require calorie counting on a day-to-day basis. Unless you are fond of tracking numbers, calorie counting does not work.

5.   Connect with nature: Spend time with nature. Nature has immense healing potentials. Find a garden and forest around you. Walk in the garden, look at the flowers, talk to the trees, get amused at the wonderful birds nature has given us.

On weekends, and sometimes during the weekdays, you may find me at the birding hotspots in Nagpur, usually around some lake, or in some garden or forest. I carry my DSLR with a powerful 600 mm prime lens and my binoculars. It is invigorating to sight colourful birds and butterflies. They never cease to surprise me with their antics.

The sounds of the forest, the scent of the trees, the sunlight playing through the leaves, the fresh, clean air — these things give us a sense of comfort. They ease our stress and worry, help us relax, and to think more clearly. Being in nature can restore our mood, give us back our energy and vitality, refresh and rejuvenate us.

The Japanese call it shinrin-yoku. Shinrin in Japanese means "forest," and yoku means "bath." So shinrin-yoku means bathing in the forest atmosphere or taking in the forest through our senses. Even a small amount of time in nature can impact our health. A two-hour forest bath will help you unplug from technology and slow down. It will bring you into the present moment and de-stress and relax you.

6. Learn: Consume quality content and information. Let knowledge come to you from all sources, but be careful of the quality of contents you consume. Filter out time-wasting contents. Read all that you can. Reading broadens your mind like no other thing. Successful people read a lot. Warren Buffett spends five to six hours a day reading five newspapers and 500 pages of corporate reports. Bill Gates reads 50 books a year. Mark Zuckerberg aimed to read at least one book every two weeks. Elon Musk grew up reading two books a day. Mark Cuban reads for over three hours every day. Arthur Blank, a co-founder of Home Depot, reads two hours a day. Billionaire entrepreneur David Rubenstein reads six books a week. Dan Gilbert, the self-made billionaire who owns the Cleveland Cavaliers, reads for one to two hours a day. Do you need more proof?

Quality books, audio-books, documentaries, online courses/lectures, and podcasts are a great way to learn. There is no learning to be had from social media.

Chapter 27 Investment is Easy to Understand

Equities: Investment" seems like a complicated thing even to a highly qualified professional. Remove the frills and the jargon, and investment becomes the simplest thing to understand. There are only two ways in which you can invest your money. You can be the owner or the lender. If you are the owner, the risks are yours, so are the rewards; when you lend, you are guaranteed a return, the owner bears the risk. The owner takes complete responsibility. He expects to get a risk premium, his return in the normal course must be higher than that of the lender. Risk thus correlates with reward, the higher the risk the higher is the reward.

Based on these criteria, you can now define each investment as ownership or lending. When you start a company investing your money and taking a loan from a bank, you are the owner; the bank is the lender. You must pay the fixed interest to the bank on the amount of loan taken, what remains after all other expenses have been paid off is your profit. Thus while a lender gets the interest or any other contractual amount, the owner gets the profit.

Now things are as easy as A-B-C. When you buy an equity share of a company, you become part-owner of the company (your ownership interest being 1 divided by the total number of shares issued by the company). If the company makes higher profits, your share in profit goes up. In a year the company makes a loss, you also lose (However your maximum loss cannot exceed the par value of your share, thanks to a modern world fiction called 'limited liability') Buying shares is thus ownership.

When you buy a bond, you get a fixed return, irrespective of the amount of profit or losses the company makes, you are thus a lender.

Mutual funds that invest in equities (another name for shares) make you proxy owners, while mutual funds that invest in debt bonds make you a lender. The mutual funds which invest partly in equity and partly in debt make you an owner to the extent of the equity portion in the total basket.

It is the owner who keeps the profits. If you want your investment to grow at an inflation-beating higher rate of growth, equity is the best option. The following section shall attempt to explain the basic concepts. Let me reiterate, things are not complicated, they have been made to look complicated. Just stick to basics and you won't go wrong.

The biggest mistake of investors is to think of a share as an instrument independent of and unrelated to the business it represents. The stock derives its value from the underlying business and what you are buying when you buy a share of a billion rupee company is one part of the ownership of the company.

You become the owner of the company to the extent of the money invested by you in the company. This is not an academic conclusion but something that has a great impact on your investment decision.

To understand the valuation process and the concept of ownership, you will apply the same criteria as you would when buying a small business across the lane. Let us say there is a small ready-made clothes store in your neighbourhood up for sale. (We will use this example to understand the concept and apply the principles learnt to buy a share in a listed large company.)

The owner approaches you with an offer to sell it to you for Rs. 50 lakh. There are two different ways you can value this business. First, you will sum up the market value of all its assets, and reduce the liabilities from it. Let us say, the value of the shop is Rs. 20 lakh, the business has a stock of goods worth Rs. 30 lakh, and has cash and cash equivalents of Rs. 10 lakh. This totals up to Rs 60 lakh. Against this, there is a bank loan of Rs. 20 lakh, thus the net sum of all assets is Rs. 40 lakh.

Why would you pay Rs 50 lakh for something worth only Rs 40 lakh? There is an invisible factor not reflected in the financial books, which is the key determinant here, the goodwill of the business. This is the best shop in the locality, and the owner is known to be an honest and sincere businessman who sells quality stuff. The owner knows every customer personally. Shopping here is a pleasant experience, and the customer loves to come back to this shop. Since our tool is inadequate to give the right valuation to this business, let us try an alternate way.

You may ask a question, how much will I earn every year if I invest Rs. 50 lakh in this business, or in short, what is my Return on Investment (ROI)? From the books of accounts you find that last year the owner earned a post-tax income of Rs. 5 lakh, thus your ROI is 10%, which looks like a fair amount. You find that the net income has been flourishing and during the past three years, it has grown from Rs 4 lakh to Rs 4.50 lakh to Rs 5 lakhs (I am keeping it simple to explain the point). Presuming that the income for the next year will be the same as the current year (Conservative estimate, since there could be disruption because of a change of ownership) by paying Rs 50 lakh you are paying 10 times the earning. Your Price to Earning Ratio, known as P/E ratio is 50:5 or 10:1 or simply 10(also called P/E multiple when expressed as a single number instead of a ratio) This in simple terms means that other things being equal (they won't be, they should improve) your payback period is 10 years, or to put it in other words, you will recover your investment in 10 years out of income that accrues to you every year.

This concept of P/E is crucial to your understanding of investment valuation. The higher the P/E ratio, the more will be the time it will take for you to recover your investment. Some stocks are fancily priced, it is not unusual to find a P/E multiple of 100 sometimes. In simple terms, you will take 100 years to get your money back. (It is not as simple as that, there are more variables, like an increase in future earnings, that need to be factored in, yet this gives you a fair idea of the utility of P/E as an important determinant of your investment decision.)

By now you know a big business does not differ from a small one regarding valuation method, as long as you apply the ownership test, i.e., you treat yourself as the owner of the business, even when you are buying just one share out of 10 million floating in the market.

Let us take the same example a step further to explain more concepts. You find this an attractive deal, but don't have money to pay to the owner. You circulate the idea of investment among your friends, and 9 of your friends will come forward and be your partners in this business, each contributing 1/10 of the required capital, i.e., Rs. 5 lakh. Now there are 10 shareholders with an investment of Rs 500,000 each. However, some of your investor friends would like to further divide their ownership into even lower units so they can invite some of their family members to invest. Since it may become too complex because of so many divisions, you all agree to split the required capital into 50,000 shares of Rs. 100 each (thus totalling to Rs 50 lakh) Now things are easy. Someone who wants to invest only 2,00,000 will be allotted 2000 shares, and one who wants to invest Rs. 1,00,000 will be allotted 100 shares, and so on. This is how share capital is split in a joint-stock company. (This explains why it is called a joint-stock company.)

Having divided capital into shares, now we can do all our analyses based on one share. Current year earnings of Rs. 5,00,000 translates into an earning per share of Rs 10 since there are 50,000 shares. We know this as EPS in the stock market language. Bingo! Things are so easy, they looked so confusing before. EPS is Rs. 10 and the market price of this share is Rs. 100, the P/E ratio is thus 10:1 (We also calculated the same ratio by using global figures.)

EPS and P/E ratio are the two factors you will keep a watch on. This is a simple but very effective tool. It helps you compare the earnings (and P/E multiple) of the company with its peers, or with the industry average. The P/E ratio is portable and can be taken out of the industry your company operates in, to be compared with the ratio of another company in an entirely different business group. You may also use P/E for comparing the performance of the same company over a different period. A higher P/E ratio means that investors wish to pay a higher price for the same amount of earnings. It may also mean that the stock has become expensive. A low P/E may mean that investors are estimating future earnings to be lower, and so the resultant multiple is lower. It may also mean that the security is undervalued, and there is a potential that stock to rise to reach its realistic P/E ratio. Thus, P/E when coupled with other tools can be an important factor for an investor to know of.

If you have come this far, you have learnt all that you need to learn. Rest is 'elementary, my dear Dr. Watson', to quote Sherlock Holmes.

Spend some time understanding equities, no other form of investment can beat equities in terms of return on investment, ease of investing, and time required to liquidate your investment.

Derivatives: While I recommend long term investment in equities as the best investment, derivatives do not qualify to be called an investment. Derivatives in the equity market mean artificial instruments that are created for trading. A derivative derives its value from the value of the underlying asset. They are traded as Futures and Options (F&O). Without getting into technical details, let me state that derivatives are dangerous instruments. They are lethal because of leverage, which means you can buy a lot by paying a very little margin. If you make a profit on your deal, it may be many times your investment, but when you lose, you may lose everything. Win-big-lose-big is not a sure way of getting rich; it is a recipe for disaster. In equity shares the highest that you can lose (theoretically, this is not likely to happen ever) is the amount of money you had invested; in derivatives, the loss may be many times bigger than your investment. You may go belly up. Derivatives are a strict no in our plan of things.

Real Estate: Real estate is ownership. Like equities, you have unlimited growth potentials.

Mark Twain once said, 'Buy land, they are not making it anymore". The greed to own land has existed since times immemorial. Kings have fought wars to gain more land and to defend their territories. A distinction has always been made between the people who own land and the people who do not. The landlords have always been the ruling class who consider themselves superior to the tenants. This has made us greedy for land. Until recently we carried the notion we never lose money in real estate. The greed for real estate created a big bubble that burst a few years back, and the investors are yet to recover from the shock. Thousands of flats are lying unsold. Builders have defaulted, many of them are bankrupt. The bubble has burst. COVID 19 pandemic has killed whatever green shoots that were trying to emerge.

Though the market will recover, real estates are still not the best of investments. Till a few years back when financial markets were not very developed, people invested in gold and real estate. Unaccounted money, which goes by the euphemism 'black money' is the key feature of the Indian economy. What better avenue to put your money in than gold and real estate? Till recently it was not uncommon for the seller to use the terms such as 60:40, which meant 60% 'white money' and 40% 'black money'. Things have changed a great deal over time though still, the sector remains a parking place for the unaccounted money.

Contrary to what people believed, long-term returns on real estate have been less than the interest on fixed deposits. Excess short-term returns were possible during periods of irrational exuberance. The collapse of the market has shattered that myth.

A key criterion to gauge the intrinsic value of the real estate is the rent it derives. In India the ratio of annual rental value to property price is low. The payback period based on rent is long, which makes real estate an unviable asset class.

Gains come from capital appreciation, and not from rent. Capital appreciation is random and erratic. Some properties may appreciate because of proximity to the market or for whatever reasons while others may not appreciate it as much. It is a gamble. This book moves its readers away from gamble and speculation. It is speculative, however good it may be. We do not recommend it.

Among all asset classes, the most illiquid is the real estate. Laws in India are complicated, the government records are far from perfect, impersonation and forged signatures were not too uncommon in the past; many properties continue to be tainted because of past bad transactions. Though procedures have improved in recent times, still the past defects continue. The sale of properties requires clearance from dozens of authorities. The typical period of realisation of sale proceeds is one year. Litigations and non-receipt of NOC's from authorities may extend this period indefinitely. Money from properties may not become available to you when you need it.

Real estates cause much of the family litigations that happen in India. Litigations continue for generations. I know of a property dispute that is pending in the courts for over a hundred years. Properties carry a bundle of emotions, nostalgia, and egos with them. Most property disputes are ego-driven and may defy logic.

Property maintenance cost is high. Taxes and supervision costs are high. Encroachment on vacant properties is common, and the cost of keeping a property free from encroachment and encumbrance is exorbitant unless you are occupying the property.

Sale price is a matter of haggling, there is no quote of the prevailing price, unlike shares and other securities where you can find the current market price on a day-to-day basis. Deals are done through a broker, often in secrecy. After the contract is executed, you discover that unscrupulous brokers have taken you for a ride.

The property does not come in small pieces, and you need larger capital investment. In Mumbai, the minimum price for the smallest apartment starts at Rs 1 crore. In comparison, you can buy shares at as low as Rs 500.

The bottom line: real estate is not a worthy investment proposition. You should consider real estate as an investment only if you can put them to actual use. If you do not own a house, buying a house is a recommended property investment for you. Buying factory land and building, office space, shops for your actual business requirements is recommended advice. Stay away from real estate for any other reason.

Gold: Gold is ownership, but is it a worthwhile investment?

The intelligent investor does not buy gold, it has no intrinsic value. The love for gold is so deep-rooted in Indian minds that whatever arguments you give people feel gold is a worthwhile investment class. Let us debunk the myth. What we talk about gold here applies to all metals and stones.

The traditional Indian view has a root in the times when the banking system was not developed and was not accessible to all, and there were not enough investment avenues. People trusted metal more than anything else. It was easy to store, and carry, and could be sold or pawned when you ran out of money. Women were happy to flaunt the jewellery. In the minds of most people in our country, gold has continued to be the most solid investment, the value of which would never go down to zero.

The reason gold is not to be considered as an investment is that gold produces no return. It has no intrinsic value, it fetches the price based on demand and supply. If the investors were to shift to gold as their favourite investment, its price will shoot up, but if the investors found another metal, say platinum, more attractive, and sold gold to buy platinum, its price would plummet.

Gold performs no economic function, it is static wealth. It has a negative intrinsic value: the investor pays storage charges to safeguard gold. It does not contribute to the economy and the nation-building. When you buy shares of a company you are transferring your savings to a company that will use the money to create value, which will generate employment, pay taxes to the government, produce goods and services which will be consumed by the economy, and so on. Gold performs no such function, your wealth lies static, producing no real gain.

"You could take all the gold that's ever been mined, and it would fill a cube 68 feet in each direction. For what that's worth at current gold prices, you could buy all—not some—of the farmland in the U.S. Plus, you could buy 16 Exxon Mobils, plus have $1 trillion of walking-around money. Or you could have a big cube of metal. Which would you take? Which will produce more value?", says Warren Buffett. On another occasion, he says, "Gold gets dug out of the ground in Africa, or someplace. Then we melt it down, dig another hole, bury it again and pay people to stand around guarding it. It has no utility. Anyone watching from Mars would be scratching their head."

"The major asset in this category is gold, currently a huge favourite of investors who fear almost all other assets, especially paper money (of whose value, as noted, they are right to be fearful). Gold, however, has two significant shortcomings, being neither of much use nor procreative. True, gold has some industrial and decorative utility, but the demand for these purposes is both limited and incapable of soaking up new production. Meanwhile, if you own one ounce of gold for an eternity, you will still own one ounce at its end."

"What motivates most gold purchasers is their belief that the ranks of the fearful will grow. During the past decade, that belief has proved correct. Beyond that, the rising price has on its own generated additional buying enthusiasm, attracting purchasers who see the rise as validating an investment thesis. As 'bandwagon' investors join any party, they create their own truth - for a while."

As for those who would still like to buy gold because it appreciates, it would interest to know as per a study, over 35 years in India, gold grew at a pathetic rate of 2.54%, silver at even lower than that at 1.35%, while equity had a double-digit rate of growth.

If you have access to modern financial systems, never invest in gold. If you live in a village which is not yet electrified, and where mobile phone and Internet do not exist, gold can be a great investment. Gold is a great alternate currency. You would recall the demonetisation announcement on 8th Nov 2016 when the first thing people did was to run to the jeweller to convert unaccounted cash into unaccounted gold. But if you are a part of the formal economy and modern financial systems, gold is not for you. Gold does not generate cash, it is not a money-making machine.

Cryptocurrencies: I am considered an expert on cryptocurrencies and am often asked to deliver talks on the future of Bitcoins and other cryptocurrencies.

In one of the talks, the auditorium was packed to capacity. The audience was eager to hear my analysis. I disappointed many when I said the true value of Bitcoins was a big ZERO. I received a series of invitations from various organisations requesting my speech on the topic. I checked on YouTube and the Internet. The dissenting voices were few. Just two or three experts saying that cryptocurrencies were a bubble. All others agreed that Bitcoins was a game-changer and predicted the price based on some matrix they used.

The true intrinsic value of any cryptocurrency is CIPHER. Not a penny more. Cryptocurrencies in 2020 are what the Internet was in 1990, and what tulips were in 1634! Few understood the Internet in the 1990s, nor many understood why tulips were so expensive in the 17th century. Few understand cryptocurrencies. People still invest. A fool and his money are soon parted. When a bubble builds up, sane voices are seldom heard.

The biggest scam of the century: the diamond industry: Diamonds are no better than cryptocurrencies as an investment. The moment we speak of diamonds, "Diamonds are forever" echos in our minds. The engagement rings must be diamond rings. It was not so just a few years back. It all started in 1938 when De Beers ran a massive campaign in the USA bringing diamonds into the culture. Public memory is short, diamonds have not been forever, they won't be forever. They have been creating a demand for diamonds the world over as the only stone that can express romance.

A diamond is a depreciating asset masquerading as an investment. Diamonds have no intrinsic value. Try selling a piece of diamond and you will recognise how illiquid it is. You may get a fraction of what you paid for buying it. Since diamonds have no intrinsic value, the sales are backed by heavy promotions and exorbitant retailer margins. The typical markup of retailer ranges from 100% to 200%. (You should realise this when your favourite jeweller offers you a 30% discount on diamond jewellery)There is a series of middlemen involved between De Beers and you, each adding his markup.

I am not getting into unethical aspects of diamond trade here (blood diamonds, bonded labour, child labour, unhealthy working conditions in the mines, etc) but am considering a pure investment angle.

Diamonds are not fungible which means they cannot be exchanged with each other. You will need to sell it at a fraction of the price if you want to buy another. So let us be clear, diamond is not an investment. Do not fall a victim to the scam.

Paintings, antiques, watches, horses, and other collectibles: A distinction must be made between assets which generate cash-flows, and those which do not. Paintings and other collectibles do not have any economic function to perform and do not generate any cash flows. They need to be maintained. They need to be insured and stored safely. Vintage cars cost a hell of a lot of money to maintain. Horses need a hefty daily allowance to maintain.

Like beauty that lies in the eyes of the beholder, the price of these assets also lies in the minds of the buyer. Painting with the signature of M.F. Hussain may sell for US$1 million. It has no relationship to the cost, there is no intrinsic value, except perhaps the money spent on paint and canvas.

We are not interested in anything that has no intrinsic value and does not perform any economic function. Since these assets have no intrinsic value, there is no benchmark price. If there is no buyer, or if the preference changes, they won't sell. Not within our domain, let's stay away from the ego products.

Chapter 28 The First Steps

Many new investors want to know where to start. What steps do they need to get going? This chapter will help you kick-start your investment.

To buy shares and mutual funds, you need to have the following accounts:

1. A DEMAT account
2. A share trading account
3. A bank account linked to the share trading account.

DEMAT Account is an account that is used to hold shares and securities in electronic format. The purpose of opening a DEMAT account is to hold shares that have been bought or dematerialised (converted from physical to electronic shares), thus making share trading easy for the users during online trading.

In India, the DEMAT account service is provided by depositories such as NSDL and CDSL through intermediaries / Depository Participant / Stock Broker. The charges of DEMAT account vary as per the volume held in the account, type subscribed, and the terms and conditions laid by the depository and the stockbroker.

A trading account is an investment account that holds securities, cash, and other holdings like any brokerage account. With a trading account, an investor can buy and sell assets. Without a trading account, you cannot trade in the stock markets. You register for an online trading account with a stockbroker or a firm. Each account comes with a unique trading ID, which is used for conducting transactions. Also, each broker offers different trading account features. Most banks also offer DEMAT account and share trading account as a part of their share trading package.

You need a bank account with Internet banking enabled to buy your investments.

Once you have all three accounts in place, you are ready to buy your investments. Transfer money from your bank account to the share trading account. Buy shares, which will get delivered electronically to your DEMAT account. When you sell shares, they will be withdrawn from your DEMAT account and transferred to the stock exchange. After the 'payout' money will get credited into your bank account. Isn't it easy?

It will be a worthwhile investment to learn the right way of investing in equity. Read the author's book "Loads of Money, Guide to Intelligent Stock Market Investing" which has helped many invest successfully in the stock market. If you are not comfortable in stock market investing, you may start with a low amount, and gradually learn the tricks. While you try to learn the game, you may start investing in an index fund or pure equity funds, which are a proxy way of investing in the stock market, and may be considered as the next best alternative.

Chapter 29 Diversify

When you carry only one stock in your portfolio, you trust all your eggs in one basket. Any fall in the price of the scrip will hit you. If your software export company is quoted at Rs 100 and the auditor of the company qualifies the Financial Statements; as a knee-jerk reaction your scrip falls to Rs 80, one remark has wiped off 20% of your capital. The solution is to diversify. However, not all risks can be mitigated by diversification.

While diversification may help you mitigate the 'specific risk', it does not mitigate the 'market risk'. The specific risk is peculiar to a company, or a small group of companies. The good news is that the specific risk is diversifiable. Statistics say just by owning two stocks you have eliminated the specific risk of owning one stock by 46 percent. Four stocks will reduce your risk by 72 percent, 16 stocks by 93 percent, and 500 stocks by 99 percent.

It does not matter if the above statistics are accurate or not, however, they bring out an important principle. As you move from one stock to two, you reduce the risk, moving up with every stock added to your portfolio, the specific risk reduces, but beyond a number around 20 stocks, the gain is not substantial. Thus, while owning 500 stocks will nearly eliminate your specific risk, it will not be a prudent thing to do. Let us see why?

While buying two stocks instead of one has reduced your risk by 46 percent, it has also reduced the reward ratio to that extent. Taking the example further, if a sudden improvement in the results of your stock causes the price to rise by Rs 20, your gains on a Rs 100 stock will be 20%, however, if you had diversified into another company and were now holding one share of the other company, let us say, priced again at Rs 100, a rise of Rs 20 in the price of your first stock would now translate into a 10% gain in your portfolio instead of 20%.

Diversification is desirable as long as the mitigation of risk arising out of diversification outweighs the dilution in appreciation that may happen because of diversification. A number between 10 and 20, depending upon your risk appetite, and the sectors and the company you invest in, should be an optimum diversification. Most investors tend to diversify so much that your portfolio looks like a miniature model of the whole market, a poor strategy. Worst, when your diversification is in inferior quality stocks, your basket has only rotten apples, and would under-perform even the indices, and may be called "diworsification".

Diversification does not mitigate market risk. Market risk is the possibility of a loss occurring to an investor which is caused by the performance of the overall market. Market risk is the systematic risk in the sense it affects the entire system. Sources of market risk include recessions, political turmoil, changes in interest rates, natural disasters, and terrorist attacks. This risk cannot be eliminated, though it can be hedged against.

Templeton versus Buffett

The successful investor, Sir John Templeton says, "Diversify. In stocks and bonds, as in much else, there is safety in numbers."; equally successful investor Warren Buffett takes the opposite view and says, "Wide diversification is only required when investors do not understand what they are doing."

Mark Twain says, 'Behold, the fool saith, "Put not all thine eggs in the one basket" - which is but a matter of saying, "Scatter your money and your attention"; but the wise man saith, "Put all your eggs in the one basket and - WATCH THAT BASKET .'

Other successful investors like George Soros, William J. O'Neil and Bernard Baruch are also known to recommend a concentrated position.

So what's the right approach? Buffett himself recommends that passive investors who do not have time or inclination to research the stocks would be better off by investing in indices. An index is nothing but a bundle of shares, so investing in indices means a broad diversification. This may look like a contradiction, but it is not. If you can understand the business so well, you can trust all your eggs in that basket, you may do that; but if you do not, spread them in different baskets. Investors like Warren Buffett have acumen and resources to know a business inside out, and can afford less diversification; but for retail investors, what we discussed earlier sounds logical, diversifying in about 20 stocks.

Diversify less, and you must have the acumen to watch that basket carefully, one rotten egg, and the valuation is severely impaired. One star performer may bring about fantastic returns on your investment. This approach is more suitable to larger investors who have resources to attend to each of the conference calls of companies they own and can keep track of every single piece of information concerning those companies.

If you diversify too broadly, as explained above, you are becoming something similar to the index, and your chance of beating the index is bleak. If you diversify too much, it becomes impossible to keep track of the updates about each of the stocks you own, and you end up becoming a passive investor, a mirror of the index fund. Diversification to the extent of around 20 companies is ideal, you may track each company. Reading 20 financial statements every year, and as many results every quarter is no big deal and is easily doable.

My strategy is to buy about 20 stocks in unrelated sectors. When one sector-*let us say technology*- is on the rise, the speculators would often square up their holdings in another sector which seems slow- *let us call it FMCG*- and pour it over the momentum. This fuels further rise in the technology sector, causing a fall in FMCG. When the reversal of trend happens, the money would flow out of technology, and get into some other sector that is rising. Diversification across sectors provides a balance against this sectoral bias. Since we invest in a few securities, the number of companies we invest in must be evenly distributed across sectors, though sometimes we may find two or three companies in a particular sector which are attractive investments.

Diversification is a matter of individual choice, more knowledgeable investors may diversify less, an average investor should diversify sufficiently, say 20 stocks, to mitigate the effect of a couple of bad investments.

Chapter 30 Manage your own investment

Experts will tell you that managing your investment is an intricate job and requires professional competence. My advice to you is to manage your own investments. Learn to do that at an early age. When you learn to invest early you will make mistakes early and will learn to get over them. The mistakes at the earlier phase of your career are cheap since you may not have much to invest. You will learn to overcome the follies quickly and cheaply.

Professional money managers charge a hefty fee- usually upfront- for managing your money. They must also deduct your share of overheads- high rentals, the salary of expensive B-school graduates, and executive perks, among others. This reduces the amount to be invested. Remember the power of compound interest. When out of Rs 100 you hand over to the money manager they deduct Rs 10, they will be investing Rs 90 instead of Rs 100. Project this over 20 years, the difference could be substantial.

However qualified the money manager may be, know that nobody has more interest in the growth of your money than you alone. Learn everything you can about the stock market, equity, mutual funds, and other investment options. Learn about long term investments. Read books on investment strategies. Read biographies of successful investors like Warren Buffett, Charlie Munger, Sir John Templeton, Phil Fisher, and others. Read Economic Times, Business Standard, Financial Express, and the Hindu Business Line. Browse business websites like Bloomberg, Investopedia, and Money Control. Read the financial statements of the companies you want to invest in. Read, read, read. Develop a passion for reading. You will thank me for this one suggestion.

Never invest your money with friends and family. If a family member or a friend approaches you with an investment proposal, know how to say no. Sometimes you may have a genuine desire to help that person, go ahead and help him, but consider it as a gift to them, not as a loan. If the money comes back to you, thank your good fortune, if it does not, don't get surprised. Consider it as having given without any intention of return right from day one. If you apply this criterion, you will be able to evaluate better the amount you should part with. If you do not have any amount that you cannot afford to lose, learn to say no.

There is a famous phrase said by Polonius in Act-I, Scene-III of William Shakespeare's play, Hamlet. The character Polonius counsels his son Laertes before he embarks on his visit to Paris. He says,

"Neither a borrower nor a lender be;
For loan oft loses both itself and friend."

It means do not lend or borrow money from a friend because if you do so, you will lose both your friend and your money. If you lend, he will avoid paying back, and if you borrow you will fall out of your savings, as you turn into a spendthrift, and face humiliation.

If giving of a loan is unavoidable, do the documentation. Make a written contract. If the borrower feels bad about it, let it be. It is your money you are parting with, and you have all the rights to protect it.

Chapter 31 "Rule No. 1: Never Lose Money

Rule No. 1: Never lose money. Rule No. 2: Never forget rule No. 1. The two end of the spectrum are: *first,* the people who take reckless risks, consider the stock market to be a get-rich-quick machine; *second,* people whose only aim in life is to protect their capital, keep it safe and secured, even if that means a lower return on investment. It is the latter category we discuss here. Ironically, in the former category, people who take an unwarranted risk, burn their fingers, and become so defensive they often shift to the other extreme of the spectrum.

Rs 100 invested in government bonds for 20 years at a compounding rate of 6% per annum will grow to Rs 320 before adjusting for taxes. Reduce taxes, and the amount would be much lower. Take into consideration the rate of inflation, and you soon realise you have been taken for a ride. Your money has grown only marginally if the rate of inflation has been low; if the inflation rate is higher, perhaps inflation has eaten into your capital and what is left is less than what you had invested.

Equity has been growing historically in India at 13-14% per annum over a 20 years window. The amount of Rs 100 invested in equity over the same period would have grown to Rs 1150 (taking 13% compounding). Tax incidence on equity being much lower, and applicable only at the point of the exit, you can appreciate the difference between the two kinds of investment.

Chasing wealth recklessly may lead you to disaster, chasing safety is no less precarious. Disaster in chasing safety is quantifiable and is certain. **The biggest risk is not taking any risk.** The intelligent investor understands that when he invests in profitable companies and stays invested for a long period, the longer he stays invested, the more he can mitigate the risk. For him risk and return cease to be two contradictory terms. He can defy the conventional wisdom that higher the risk lower is the return, he can now operate in an environment of low risk, and high return.

Not that prudence is bad. Certainly not. Safety is your goal, but know that safety does not mean parking your money in securities which promise the return of capital but do not grow. The equity market is volatile in the short run, and your investments may fall by 20% in just a few days. You cannot time the market and may buy at the peak where the prices may not hold for a long and may head south after you buy it. There are years when the market continues to be low. Worse, there are years where the market continues to fall. You should invest more, not less, during such periods of uncertainty. The best time to buy is when there is blood in the market. Buy when everybody else is selling and sell when everybody else is buying, and you will stand out as an intelligent investor. Be fearful when others are greedy and be greedy when others are fearful.

India is a robust economy, growing faster than most other economies in the world, and is likely to grow at a steady pace over the next 10, 20, or 30 years. Short-term hiccups will occur, and they might prove to be a setback to the market, but know that the long-term trend is positive, and the country will continue to grow stronger. Those short-term hiccups are not to be looked upon as impediments to wealth creation, they are an opportunity for greater wealth creation.
People will continue to panic at every bad news; the intelligent investor must use that panic as an opportunity. Every intelligent investor should remember these words as the gospel truth: ***Be fearful when others are greedy and be greedy when others are fearful.***

Holding shares for a long period evens out fluctuations, and the low years are likely to be an advantage to you, and if you extend the holding period of your investment to a period beyond 10 years, the stock becomes as safe as bonds, and if you extend it beyond 20 years, stock turns to be safer than any other investment.
This is the reason, you should be investing early on, stay invested with a

longish term perspective, and since you will invest with a long time horizon, your investment should be in businesses that continue to grow over a long period. This eliminates penny stocks and companies with uncertain business models or businesses with poor quality management.

You are not buying tickers, you are not buying 'tips', you are buying a thin slice of ownership in a great business. If you are to hold to an investment for the long-term, you would need to test the business the same way a potential owner of a business would do. You will examine the cash flow, return on capital employed, the ratio of debt to equity, and a few more ratios, much like the owner of the business would do. We will discuss the key financial analysis in another chapter, and it is easy and requires nothing more than basic arithmetical skills. Here it would suffice to say you need to have an owner's mindset when you buy your shares. Amount to be invested notwithstanding. The criteria remain the same for a Rs 1000 investment, and Rs one million investment.

Chapter 32 Investment Rules

The pursuit of wealth without the right tools and temperament makes many of the first-time investors vulnerable. The other extreme is more than unwarranted caution, the quest for security. While the younger investors fall for the former, we often see the older ones obsessed with the latter. Mindless pursuit of wealth is risky as throwing a die, the outcome may or may not be favourable, and if one round of throwing die wins the game for you, it does not mean that in the next round you will win again.

Extreme caution makes you so much risk-averse, that you invest in government bonds, not realising that while your capital is guaranteed in government bonds, the return is sometimes lower than the rate of inflation, so while you take back your Rs. 100,000 after 10 years, you realise that inflation has eroded the value of your money, and Rs 1,00,000 that you received with a smile on your face is much less than Rs 1,00,000 that you had invested.

Most of the newbies on the stock market think more activity means more return. They swing at every ball thrown to them, and the more they miss the balls, the more fervently they play. The more they play, the more it hurts. They find 'penny stocks' attractive because a stock selling at Rs. 3 yesterday might rise to Rs. 5 today, giving unbelievable returns, which seems too good to be true. In the long run, that return is too good to be true because it does not exist. The net consequences of buying penny stocks at the end of the year are unpredictable, it is akin to a lottery, with the probability of loss is higher than gain. By trading frequently, you end up making more money for your broker than for yourself.

Brokers are happy to have clients who are impulsive and buy and sell at every noise that happens on CNBC. My broker tells me he makes 10 times more money in commission from someone who has invested 1/5th of my investment- a difference of 50 times-because that investor trades every day and every churn of your capital must put a smile on the face of your broker.

The government is also happy with the guy who trades frequently: the profits from short-term gains are taxed at a higher rate. Long-term investors pay a reduced rate of tax, which they pay when they exit a particular investment. In effect, they are reinvesting the money saved from brokerage, and the tax money, resulting in a higher return when compounded over a long period. Some of them- as I do- would defer the tax payment almost indefinitely, as my favourite investment period is forever.

Not to say all stockbrokers and investment advisers are bad or ill-intentioned people. The problem is with the basic characteristic of the market: frequent trading is the norm, rather than an exception. It is the investor who has to decide on his investment method. Buy and hold seems unglamorous in a world where information is delivered in a Nano-second from one part of the globe to another, and in a supposedly efficient market, every information is said to be factored in in real-time in the price quotation, and the temptation is to buy and sell at the point where a piece of new information is getting factored in the price quote. These frequent transactions are good for the market: number of buyers, number of sellers, frequent trading, transparent trading platform all lead to Adam Smith's model of a perfect market.

However, one must understand that a perfect market does not make it efficient. Irrationality is the key feature of the market, and it is this feature that makes the market attractive for a long-term investor.

You need to have certain traits to be a successful investor. Your character, traits, and behaviour will be put to the severest test in the market. You need to have patience, common sense, perseverance, humility, foresight, a desire to succeed, detachment, mindfulness, a quest for knowledge, and an ability to admit your mistakes and learn from them. Most important, you must have a belief in yourself and in this investment method. If you think I am asking for too much, I am not.

Most people already have these traits, they lie dormant in some of us. If I am your first mentor in investing through this book, nobody told you before that it pays to sit cool on your investment, instead of frantic activities. But if you know you are impulsive and shortsighted, and short-term happenings make you lose your long term focus, then I may not help. Gut feeling is the worst feeling to have in the stock market. If you feel the stock market will be up based on your gut feeling, you will soon prove yourself wrong.

Even if you prove yourself right sometimes, it is not the way to invest. Research has proved that you often go wrong when you go by perception. By the time you form your opinion, the situation has already changed. We are bad at timing the market. In a bull market, whatever you predict comes true. Because everything is rising, what you predict rises. The bull market leads to over-confidence. You believe your gut feeling always proves right, a case of mistaking correlation for causation. One day the market refuses to follow your gut and the whole edifice of paper profits you were building falls like a pack of cards.

Professional investors make the same mistake. It is interesting to find that when you talk to people about their investment philosophy; they say they are long-term investors. They are long-term investors only as long as the market is trending up, the day it falls, they panic and become short-term investors again, selling when the market is low.

We are advocating a scientific approach to discovering mis-pricing here and exploiting that to your advantage. The method is foolproof and works in all situations in the long run.

Good thing is that having these traits will make you successful not only in investing but in other areas of life and career too. It will enhance your personality and you will rise above the mediocre. Good investors are great human beings too.

Here are some important rules to follow:

1.   No investment is possible unless you save. Saving is a prerequisite. Save as much as you can, as early as you can.

2.   Of all the investment avenues we have discussed, equity shares are the best. Learn the ropes, so you don't do it the wrong way. Reading my book, "Loads of Money" and similar other books that teach you to invest for the long term is highly recommended.

3.   The long term investment is, well, long term investment. If you need some money in the short term, it may not come out of a long term investment. If you have to pay a college fee for education abroad and it falls due in 6 months, your long term investment may not help. Equity market being in a constant flux of greed and fear, you cannot predict the market direction on the day you need money. Always keep a provision for expected short-term requirements and keep it aside in liquid non-fluctuating assets.

4.   When I say long term, I mean a period of minimum 5 years. To some like Warren Buffett, and I, the holding period is eternity, I do not sell my equities unless I direly need money, or I have made a wrong investment decision, or one of my investments has fallen permanently (change of technology is an example of things that may bring about such a change). I seldom sell for any other reason.

5.   Diversify. Do not trust all your eggs in one basket. However, too much diversification makes your return lower. My ideal diversification plan is to invest in 20 stocks, and I also diversify between different sectors. Some sectors run contrary to others, diversification helps you balance. During the COVID-19 pandemic, while all other sectors have lost 20% of their value, FMCG and pharmaceuticals have gained.

6.   Ignore the day-to-day fluctuations. Long term investor does not bother about how his investment behaves in the short term. They are not glued to the screen during trading hours. They buy quality

stocks and keep them aside. Momentum trading, intraday trading selling short is not the stuff that will make you a real investor.

7.   Do not invest on tips. Stay away from fortune-tellers who sometimes show up as formal suit-wearing experts on CNBC. Do your homework. I do not invest in companies whose business model I don't understand. I do not buy stocks of companies that have not been making profits for 10 years continuously. I look at the PE ratio and look for the debt component in the company's balance sheet. I do not buy a heavily indebted company.

8.   Do not time the market. You cannot. Good stocks are available in all market conditions. It is only in retrospect that you will know if the market was high or low. You are too small a player in the compared to the market size to time it.

9.   Learn to be a contrarian. Learn to buy when others are selling. The market is manic depressive, it suddenly quotes too high or too low; buy when it is quoting low. Be fearful when others are greedy and be greedy when others are fearful.

10.   Trade less. Money is made by sitting on your stocks. If you frequently churn your portfolio, you are making money for your stockbroker.

11.   Your health, happiness, and relationships are the highest priority investments. Nurture them carefully, and place them on the top of your list.

Chapter 33 The Mindset of an Investor

The investor's chief problem—and even his worst enemy—is likely to be himself". Investment is as much about psychology as it is about economics. People often fail in the former. World-class economists don't make world-class investors, many of them are the worst performers. Investment success depends on the mental makeup of the investor combined with technical competence.

Few know Albert Einstein invested much of his 1921 Nobel Prize money in stock markets. However, he lost bulk in the stock market crash in 1929. Einstein was awarded 121,572.54 Swedish kronor as Nobel Prize in Physics, which was equivalent to over twelve years' income for Albert Einstein back then. He lost almost all of it and realised that his Nobel Prize-winning wisdom was not suitable for winning in the stock market. The stock market requires a different temperament.

You are your worst enemy. Frenzy, exuberance and excesses in the market, dubious companies with window-dressed balance sheets, a sudden change in domestic and international macros may not harm you as much as your temperament.

Patience: The most important trait that an investor ought to have is patience. No matter how technically sound you are, you are likely to face rough weather, the market will go down, your investment will underperform for quite some time, and unless you have inculcated the virtue of patience, you are likely to sell at the wrong time. Lack of patience makes people do dumb things with their money.

Greed and fear are two dominating forces in the market, and unless you have trained your senses to stay disciplined in the face of such extreme market behaviours, you are likely to succumb. One factor that distinguishes Warren Buffett, Charlie Munger, Peter Lynch from other investors is the tremendous patience and discipline they have.

Buffett says he would be happy if stock markets were closed for 10 years after he bought his investments, so he would have no means to track his investments while they continue to grow. It requires nothing less than the Job's patience to hold on to your investment when the market forces are against it, and a great deal of conviction in your investment philosophy.

Munger says, "You have to be patient, wait until something comes along, which, at the price you're paying, is easy. That's contrary to human nature, just to sit there all day long doing nothing, waiting. It's easy for us, we have a lot of other things to do. But for an ordinary person, can you imagine just sitting for five years doing nothing? You don't feel active, you don't feel useful, so you do something stupid." We are not out in the market looking for investments; we are just waiting for the right investment which we have identified become available to us at the right price. Till the price comes to the level that gives enough margin of safety we wait, with our ears and eyes wide open. We keep reading everything about the potential investment. The day the right investment becomes available to us at the price we wanted to buy it at, we buy like crazy.

Investing is not cricket

In cricket, the batsman must hit every ball that is bowled to him. If he does not, either the ball would hit the stumps, or if he obstructs the stumps with his body, it would be an LBW. He has to decide at every ball how to play so he remains at the crease for a longer time and can score well when he can hit the sweet spot. The player remains under tremendous pressure, the cheering and shouting of spectators adding to the confusion.

The intelligent investor does not invest like an intelligent cricketer who plays cricket. He has an advantage over the cricketer. He need not play every ball. He can decide not to play a ball he does not understand, and it has no penalty point. He can wait for a favourable ball to come, and he can hit that ball with full force.

Warren Buffett used the baseball analogy to explain this point. He says, "The trick in investing is just to sit there and watch pitch after pitch go by and wait for the one right in your sweet spot. And if people are yelling, 'Swing, you bum!' ignore them." Buffett only invests in companies that are within his "circle of competence," a concept he first described in his 1996 Shareholder Letter. "You don't have to be an expert on every company or even many," he says. "You only have to be able to evaluate companies within your circle of competence. The size of that circle is not very important; knowing its boundaries, however, is vital."

If you stick to what you know, you would never go wrong. You don't have to buy every stock that looks interesting to you, you should have the ability to filter out the noise, and focus on the companies you can understand. Because of your education, experience, interest, research, and passion, you might have developed expertise in certain industries. Sticking to those industries would make your investment safe. You may ignore the Infosys's and Wipro's if you do not understand the technology. They may be great investment ideas, but they are not for you.

If you decide that you have to hit only 20 balls during your entire investing career, and there is no penalty for not playing a ball, you will be as careful as you can. You will buy only those companies you can understand well, else you would not hold it for a day.

If you look at the Indian market scene, it is opposite to this. People are burning off their energies and monies buying and selling stocks they don't understand, at the drop of a hat. They perhaps bought them on "tips", and would sell them when they need money for buying another "tip". End of the year when they draw the accounts for the year they find while they have been moving at a frantic pace. They travelled no distance. They end up making more money for intermediaries through commission than for themselves. We need a disciplined, systematised approach towards stock market investing.

The market is dominated by untrained traders who do not know how to control their emotions. Alternating bouts of greed and fear decide a trader's investment patterns. When buying a mobile phone, he carries out a vast amount of research about the megapixels of the camera, and the GB in RAM, and battery life. When investing he leaves it to Mr. Market to decide for him. If he were to spend half as time on his lakhs of rupees worth of investment as he spends on buying a Rs 20,000 mobile phone, he would be much better off. He cannot see stock as a share in the business and looks at it as a moneymaking proposition.

Insulation: The investor needs to inculcate the talent to turn out the noise. Tune in to CNBC and you see tickers moving up and down trying to capture every news and every piece of rumour. More often than not, the 'information' is mere noise, with no effect on the fundamentals of the stock. When the market reacts, it overreacts. Shutting down the noise will make you rise much above the average investor whose buy and sell decisions are impacted by short-term noises in the market. Some people don't want to miss a single piece of chatter and stay glued to the screen all day long. In the connected world, information travels fast and misinformation travels faster. A single WhatsApp message can bring a company down and a single Tweet may make the stock soar. The reaction is often disproportionate to the financial implication of the news.

Focus: The ability to stay on course in the face of conflicting signals is an important winning trait. Staying on course is a close cousin of patience, and intelligent investors are known not to deviate. The average investor digresses from the course because he doesn't even know what path he has chosen. He does not define his investment goals. If you do not know where you want to go, you can never reach there. Hundreds of distractions coming his way every day are likely to make him sell when he should buy, and vice versa.

The ability to stay calm in the face of a storm makes you a successful investor. When there is blood in the market, we see most people running for cover. The intelligent investor stays calm and unperturbed and is trying to find value in the market. During the frenzy, people who stay calm are likely to discover great investments, while others seem to feel the heat.

Do your homework: The intelligent investor remains patient and calm and does not succumb to noise and stays on course because of an important trait he possesses: He does his homework well. He knows why he has made a particular investment. He studies every quarterly result, half-yearly result, and annual results of the company he has invested in to know the original premise he based his decisions on is still valid; and if it is no longer valid, does it call for a change in the decision? Experience suggests that if you have done your homework well, and are satisfied with the fundamentals of the company, in a majority of cases you are likely to find a reinforcement of your belief in subsequent events.

In a few cases, you are likely to see the fundamentals deteriorate. However, if the fundamentals of one company you are invested in deteriorate beyond repair, you might exit it. Selling at this point also requires a calm mind: if fundamentals have gone off the mark, the intelligent investor would exit the scrip while the frenzy investor would wait for the share to come back to a particular price so he recovers his losses, which may prove to be a futile exercise.

The intelligent investor rarely sells his investment unless he needs money or unless he finds that fundamental assumptions are no longer valid. And when he sells it, he remains indifferent to the profit or loss made in the transaction. To him, the latter situation is nothing more than plucking out the weeds so that the rest of the farm may grow better.

Singles and Doubles, not Fours and Sixes, make you rich

If it seems too good to be true, it probably is. There is no get-rich--quick formula. Trace the history of people who made it big, and you will find one common thread: they were consistent in their money-making approach, and they consolidated on small gains. Baby steps matter. The journey of a thousand steps begins with one step. Take that step as soon as you can, then take the next step, and the next one till you reach where you want to reach. Big leap may crash you, play safe.

To use the cricket analogy, life is a test match, not a T20 which moves in a fast forward mode. The winner in the cricket of life is the batsman who scores cheeky singles and doubles at every ball and stays longer in the crease; and not the batsman who hits fours and sixes but runs out of energy and burns out soon.

Indian shares market may give you a consistent return of 12-14% pa which to some of you may look like a low rate of growth, because your speculator friend may boast of how much money he makes in a single day by buying and selling the stocks the same day. He may have an impressive show till something that suddenly disrupts the market, and all gains vanish. As I write this, the world is facing the worst pandemic in history. Share prices have plummeted to the lowest levels in decades. The slow and consistent player remains unperturbed. They know the world will not fall and this too shall pass. To them, this is an opportunity to buy quality stocks that they could not buy earlier. However, the speculator- the fast run making batsman-finds himself naked in such a situation and runs for cover.

Another example is an investor who puts his money in a new company with an unproven track record which promises to make unlimited money. While some of these companies may be multi-baggers many of them may not survive in the long run. The investor who invests in a company existing for the last 20 years, which unbroken record of making consistent profits will prove to be wiser in the long run. Stay safe and invest wisely. This is the race where the tortoise always wins over the hare. Stick with the smart, long-term, lower-risk investments.

Chapter 34 What are we Doing With our Lives?

When I see a corporate executive getting a hefty pay package come back home tired after a day's stressful work, with no energy left, spreading himself on a couch, still thinking of the month-end deadline, not able to connect with family nor with the TV show, I wonder if this was the life they wanted? The executive compensation keeps getting higher every few months, with more money comes more responsibilities. That brings more stress and less time for family and friends. If this were to bring more happiness, it could have been acceptable. It does not. Happiness often follows an inverse path with your career development. More money does not bring happiness either. If you think you are making a living, you are wrong. You are making a dying.

When I discuss personal finance with my clients and ask them what is their primary stress, the usual answer is less money. When I ask them how much more money will make them happy, the reply varies from 10% to 100% increase over the present level of income. Can you see the point here? Whatever be your present situation, you feel you will be better off by earning more money. People of all income range from Rs. 20,000 a month to Rs. 2 crores a year have the same answer: a little more than what they have. If I were to wave a magic wand and raise their income to their dream level, do you think they will live happily thereafter? They won't. The expenditure will immediately rise to meet the income available, and they will be in the same state of darkness. There is no permanent solution to this problem unless you take control of your life. Living within your means is the only way out. List out all activities that most people around you do for a week and you will be convinced they are not living for any purpose other than paying their bills.

If someone asks you "What do you do?", you are likely to reply that I am a lawyer, or an IT professional, or a student or a CA or a shopkeeper. Is your profession your only identity? We have become so obsessed with the job we do that we have stopped thinking of ourselves as composite human beings. We are focused on '9 to 5 till 65' rut. We don't realise how much this has impacted our relationships, our personality growth. We have caused irreversible damage to the environment. Has all this improved our life? All the time we think of our jobs. We compare our jobs to that of others. Jobs is the new caste system. We place people in the hierarchy base on the jobs they do. An electrician doing an intricate electrical fitting job is lower in the hierarchy than someone working on a white-collar job. The electrician might take home three times the desk job worker does, but he is thought of lower in the graph. A teacher's job is no less important in shaping a nation than that of an engineer or a doctor, but she is paid much less and is placed lower in the social hierarchy. So is a housewife whose contribution to bringing up a family is undeniably high, but is low in the caste system of jobs. We are obsessed with the job-caste system.

We are earning more and more and spending extravagantly. We are damaging the environment through our actions. As I write this in the middle of the pandemic, a surprise reversal of the environmental damage is happening in 21 days of lockdown. A few days ago, Noida's busiest Sector-18 had an unexpected guest. A Nilgai was spotted walking leisurely on the road. The sight was a welcome change from the usually jam-packed road. Similarly, in Kerala's Kozhikode, a Malabar civet, which is a critically endangered animal, was spotted walking on the road. Mother Earth seems to have rejuvenated itself – smog has given way to blue skies, marine life is seeing increased activity, pollution levels have dropped, and animals and birds are moving about on their own accord. India is home to 21 of the world's 30 most polluted cities, but recently air pollution levels have dropped dramatically. The Canals in Venice are clearer than what they have been in nearly 60 years. From Jalandhar in Punjab you can see the mountain range in Himachal Pradesh never seen in the past 30 years. Nature is reclaiming its space.

Excess money causes the most environmental blunders. We know that "wealthy" countries in Europe, North America, and parts of Asia have higher per capita environmental burdens than poorer countries and that the people of the former are living beyond the bio-physical boundaries – the limits of the environment –to do so. But those at the top levels of these countries are practising lifestyles with even higher environmental consequences, enabled by their wealth.

In an average mature economy like the UK's, the ecological footprint is 6.69 global hectares per person. That means if everybody in the world had this lifestyle we would need 3.7 planets to support us all.

The annual average personal carbon footprint is 7.3 tonnes, and yet the estimated sustainable footprint we should all have by 2050 is 1.5 tonnes per annum. Every time you fly an airplane you are adding to your carbon footprints. I am often amused to see the World Economic Forum, Davos discussing the environmental issues, the leaders from all over the world arriving by planes, many of them by private jets. Though the aim is laudable, the cost of the convention in terms of environmental damage is high. When Google convened a meeting of the rich and famous in Sicily in July to discuss climate breakdown, its delegates arrived in 114 private jets and a fleet of mega-yachts and drove around the island in super-cars. Even when they mean well, the ultra-rich cannot help trashing the living world.

Every object we add to our possessions- houses, cars, boats, clothes, jewellery, technology- impacts the environment. If this comes as news to you, try to understand the concept of Ecological Rucksacks. An Ecological Rucksack is the total quantity (in kg) of materials moved from nature to create a product or service, minus the actual weight of the product. Ecological rucksacks look at hidden material flows. Ecological rucksacks take a life cycle approach and signify the environmental strain or resource efficiency of the product or service. On average, industrial products carry non-renewable rucksacks are about 30 times their weight. Only about 5 percent of non-renewable natural material disturbed in the ecosphere typically ends up in a technically useful form. Even the present trend of buying 'green' depletes nature, though to a little less extent.

We have depleted the earth; we owe mother earth a big debt. We leeched the resources that our ancestors had left behind as sustainability measures (their lifestyle made earth sustainable) and we have also squandered away the resources that were meant for our children. We have become richer by making the earth poor, and we are using our money to make it poorer. The paradox is, the more the money we have, the more we are borrowing- not from the banks- but our children and grandchildren and great-grandchildren. We shall never repay that debt because we don't understand we are borrowing. The threat does not show immediately like the reading on a meter, so we remain complacent until the pandemic happens or air quality goes so bad that we can hardly breathe. To repeat, we are not making a living; we are making a dying.

As long as we believe in more is better we will continue to make a dying. It seldom brings happiness, it causes misery to you and the world around you. To live a happier life (which automatically leads to living an eco-friendly life) is to stay focused on consuming less, justifying each consumption and purchase, improving work/life balance, and becoming more self-sufficient. It means living a life that has simplicity and modesty as its virtues, reflection as its characteristic, letting go as its attitude. This is easy to practice in the land that draws its inspiration from the philosophies of Buddha, Mahavir, Nanak. Draw inspiration from Gandhi, the best practitioner of these virtues that the world has ever produced.

Reducing your possessions is not about physical possessions alone. Unclutter your mind. Eliminate noise around you. Look for opportunities to laugh, and laugh out loud when you get such opportunities. If it is considered uncultured to laugh out loud, so it be. Take a walk and connect with nature. Nature is the reset button.

Let go. "To let go does not mean to get rid of. To let go means to let be. When we let be with compassion, things come and go on their own.", says the author Jack Kornfield. Replaying the past repeatedly doesn't change it, and wishing things were different doesn't make it so. Learn to let go of what is hurting you, even if it seems an impossible task. You must let go to set yourself free from the bondage of the past. You cannot be what you want to be unless you empty the past baggage and let your mind wander freely in the future, not in the past. You can't change the past; you can only decide today to help how your future turns out. Learn to forgive, forget, and move forward.

Epilogue: Life after the Pandemic

Life has changed after COVID-19. The lockdown was a crash course in many important life-lessons. We learnt to slow down, to meditate, to contemplate, to spend time with ourselves, and with family. We learnt new skills, went back to basics, and rediscovered the joy of traditional food and family recipes. The long-forgotten board games and other games families played before the digital era were revived. People reconnected with the neglected segment- the elderly and differently-abled.

We learnt to live within our means. It was fashionable to speak of minimalism, but we seldom understood its import. The lockdown allowed us to practice minimalism and to unclutter our homes and our minds. We learnt to cut back on frivolous expenditure. We learnt to cook, to mend things, to find a workaround to most of our problems. It made us realise that to live you need a little money. It made us realise that money and happiness are not correlated.

Some things we did during this short period will stay with us forever. Some things will become the new normal. Life after COVID-19 will never be the same again.

Businesses got disrupted. Some of them will bounce back, some may fail to revive. We were already amid a recession, the longest and the biggest lock-down in the history- 1.3 billion people staying at home for 40 days- is leading to the contraction of the economy, something that few people of the present generation have witnessed before. There will be culling of businesses, those with leverage and heavy overheads may find it difficult to survive. The fittest will survive. Unemployment will surge. Better talents will be available at a lower cost. The top-heavy corporate salary structure will see a readjustment.

The nature of healthcare will see a dramatic change. Telemedicine will get a boost; some regulatory hurdles will be removed to make telemedicine more practical. The cost of hospitalisation will increase; the patients will be screened more effectively at the point of admission. With healthcare becoming expensive, the much neglected preventive medicine should boost.

Hygiene standards will see a dramatic change. The simple act of washing your hands may prevent many communicable diseases. In India, we neglected the basic hygiene practice. 40 days are enough to build good habits, and they will stay with us forever. This will also help reduce the incidence of normal flu and other diseases. Better practices will make future pandemics less likely and less impactful. Immunity was something we neglected in the past. The diet of the future will have more immunity-boosting ingredients. Hyper-local fruits and vegetables will find their way into your meals.

The venture funding industry and banking will revise the policy. A strong business model, quality management, agility, and lower overheads will be important criteria to finance businesses. Companies like OYO might face rough weather.

Companies will adopt innovative practices experimented with during the lockdown. ITC and HUL will tie-up with Zomato and Swiggy to deliver the daily needs directly to the consumer. Delivery companies will diversify into delivering groceries and vegetables.

Some people lived from paycheque to paycheque. They were suddenly in for a big shock. There was no money coming into the account. Post-COVID-19, people will understand the need for an emergency fund. You should have liquid resources equal to six months of expenditure. This will help you face any future crisis in your career. Digital banking will get a boost.

People learnt to work from home. The disruption was abrupt and WFH was not without its share of complications. There were data and network security risks involved, and some activities are not amenable to WFH. However, many people and businesses discovered that they can work from home without loss of productivity. In Mumbai, where rentals are high and space is a real constraint, stockbroking companies found that WFH for their employees is a more cost-effective solution. Many jobs where the outcome is measurable will move to the WFH model. Non-quantifiable work will shift back to the office.

The education model will see a sea-change. Earlier online education model was a poor substitute for the contact classes. When teachers were forced to teach online, the limitations of both models became visible. The future of education will see a combination of both offline and online models, with an optimum balance in the strengths of both.

Air travels will see a big drop initially. But this is likely to be a short-term phenomenon. After 9/11 the experts predicted that people will travel less, the air travel had dropped to less than half, but it bounced back in no time. Traditional businesses that cannot be remotely done- plumber, electrician, beautician, barber- will gain more respect and will continue without disruption.

Sharing businesses- Ola, Uber, Airbnb will take some time to bounce back. They will have to innovate to get back in business. When you check in a hotel, you find a paper cover on the toilet seat announcing that the toilet has been cleaned for your protection. Similar innovations will be required by cab and home-sharing businesses to assure you that hygiene standards are being followed.

Many of us rekindled our love for homemade food. Cloud kitchens with ammas and aajis cooking the traditional food will find many takers, to that extent making a dent in restaurant sales.

One dark horse in the crisis was Doordarshan, which was written off as dead and gone. In the age of Netflix and Amazon Prime and Hotstar, traditional TV channels can be serious competition. No amount of market research would have concluded that. The government needs to understand the strength of Doordarshan and build on it.

The relief package for the poor has been announced. There will be more relief packages in the offing. The money should be put in the pockets of the jobless and hungry. This will cause a dramatic redistribution of wealth. The money which in the normal course changes many hands before passing on to the bottom of the pyramid will directly be transferred to the bank accounts of the poor. It will not affect the upper class: to them, a fall in the total wealth has no impact except a change in paper-valuation. The poor will hopefully survive- they must survive if they collapse the country collapses. The worst sufferers will be the middle class: salary earners, people paying rent and EMI's, shopkeepers, small businesses, entrepreneurs, MSME. Their woes will need to be addressed, the Budget 2020 will need to be redesigned from scratch, it has lost its validity in the present scenario.

www.ingramcontent.com/pod-product-compliance
Lightning Source LLC
Chambersburg PA
CBHW070548220526
45467CB00003B/1116